BALLISTIC MISSILES IN MODERN CONFLICT

THE WASHINGTON PAPERS

. . . intended to meet the need for an authoritative, yet prompt, public appraisal of the major developments in world affairs.

President, CSIS: David M. Abshire

Series Editor: Walter Laqueur

Director of Publications: Nancy B. Eddy

Managing Editor: Donna R. Spitler

MANUSCRIPT SUBMISSION

The Washington Papers and Praeger Publishers welcome inquiries concerning manuscript submissions. Please include with your inquiry a curriculum vitae, synopsis, table of contents, and estimated manuscript length. Manuscripts must be between 120–200 double-spaced typed pages. All submissions will be peer reviewed. Submissions to *The Washington Papers* should be sent to *The Washington Papers*; The Center for Strategic and International Studies; 1800 K Street NW; Suite 400; Washington, DC 20006. Book proposals should be sent to Praeger Publishers; One Madison Avenue; New York NY 10010.

BALLISTIC MISSILES IN MODERN CONFLICT

W. SETH CARUS

FOREWORD BY EDWARD N. LUTTWAK

PUBLISHED WITH THE
CENTER FOR STRATEGIC AND
INTERNATIONAL STUDIES

PRAEGER

New York
Westport, Connecticut
London

Library of Congress Cataloging-in-Publication Data

Carus, W. Seth.
  Ballistic missiles in modern conflict / W. Seth Carus ; foreword
by Edward N. Luttwak.
    p. cm. – (Washington papers ; 146)
  Expanded version of: Ballistic missiles in the Third World.
  "Published with the Center for Strategic and International
Studies, Washington, D.C."
  Includes bibliographical references and index.
  ISBN 0-275-94077-2 (alk. paper)
  1. Ballistic missiles. 2. Munitions. 3. Arms control.
I. Carus, W. Seth. Ballistic missiles in the Third World.
II. Center for Strategic and International Studies (Washington,
D.C.) III. Title. IV. Series.
UG1312.B34C36   1991
358.1'7182–dc20   91-8731

British Library Cataloguing in Publication Data is available.

Library of Congress Catalog Card Number: 91-8731
ISBN: 0-275-94077-2

This is an expanded version of *Ballistic Missiles in the Third World:
Threat and Response*

First published in 1991

Praeger Publishers, One Madison Avenue, New York, NY 10010
An imprint of Greenwood Publishing Group, Inc.

Printed in the United States of America

The paper used in this book complies with the
Permanent Paper Standard issued by the National
Information Standards Organization (Z39.48-1984).

10 9 8 7 6 5 4 3 2 1

Contents

Foreword

In a very loose sense, ballistic missiles are more advanced than manned combat aircraft, yet they are much easier to employ. Given the ability to reproduce certain narrow technologies, they are also much easier to manufacture. Countries that would have great difficulty in assembling the trained array of operational, tactical, and technical specialists needed for an effective bomber force can nevertheless bombard their enemies with ready-to-fire ballistic missiles, whose guidance can be preset by a handful of technicians (easily imported if need be). And countries that could scarcely acquire, let alone staff, a jet-engine factory, an airframe plant, and the varied elements of an entire electronics industry can reproduce ballistic missiles, and even further develop imported models in much simpler industrial installations.

Above all, there is the question of range. The navigation, refueling, and protection requirements of a bombing force sharply increase with distance, so much so that there is an immediately recognizable difference between strategic bombers, deep-strike aircraft, and fighter-bombers that can only drop ordnance just across a front line. The costs of acquiring and operating each class of aircraft are dramatically different, their crews require appreciably different skills (even a somewhat different mentality), and the force that operates them must have quite different abilities, because the selection and location of targets, the planning of missions, and even the metereological forecasting acquire a different cast.

There is also a political difference. Several countries manufacture fighter-bombers of one sort or another, including China and France who have both at various times been willing to sell their aircraft to virtually any buyer with funds. Deep-strike aircraft, by contrast, are only produced by the European Tornado consortium, the Soviet Union, and the United States. Although both Britain (the chief Tornado salesman) and the Soviet Union have shown a distinct proclivity for selling to all comers with cash in hand, the high cost of these aircraft and the complexity of their upkeep have inhibited all but a handful of purchasers, some of which (for example, Libya) have been scarcely able to operate them at all. The production of strategic bombers of any efficiency is even more narrowly confined to the Soviet Union and the United States, and neither has sold any at all to third parties.

All these differences—political, technical, operational, and institutional—conjointly limit the number of air forces capable of strategic bombardment to a mere handful, as opposed to the ten or so that can carry out deep-strike raids and the dozens capable of dropping bombs at closer ranges.

These range boundaries have had an importance that far transcends the technicalities of air power. They have greatly helped to keep local wars local and regional confrontations regional. Since 1945, they have variously ensured that North Korea could not attack by air the Japanese bases and ports from which U.S. engagement in the peninsula was largely sustained; dissuaded North Vietnam from bombarding Thailand when that country was participating in the Vietnam War; prevented India and Pakistan from attacking each other's enormously vulnerable cities in 1965 and again in 1971; kept Arab-Israeli wars from harming civilians at large to an even greater extent than they did; largely incapacitated Libyan hostility when it reached culminating extremes of unbounded fury against Britain, France, Egypt, Italy, Morocco, Chad, Tunisia, and the United States at times (but did not wholly spare Sudan); and largely confined the Iran-Iraq War to frontal warfare – until each country was able to acquire ballistic missiles.

Ballistic missiles are different in this regard, too. In their case, range is largely a matter of sheer scale, except insofar as the particular targets meant for attack are small enough to call for some degree of precision (the "drift" of all inertial guidance devices increases with time, and external forms of guidance are impractical at longer ranges). Because cities and large military bases are almost the only plausible targets and precision of a high order is scarcely needed, long-range ballistic missiles differ technologically from their counterparts of lesser range only in their interstage connections and in the greater (but still incremental) refinement of their guidance apparatus (to overcome "drift"). Thus, a country that can manufacture ballistic missiles with a range of, say, 300 kilometers will not generally encounter great difficulties in producing ballistic missiles with a range of 600 kilometers and may well be able to acquire ballistic missiles with a range of 6,000 kilometers – without having to overcome the enormous barriers, both political and operational, that constitute such a secure fire wall between tactical and strategic airpower.

The diffusion of ballistic missiles is thus a matter that should concern all observers of international politics and not merely professional specialists. The spread of ballistic missiles entails the potential geographic spread of local wars and regional confrontations. Familiar categories may thus be overturned, as conflicts deemed till now strictly localized may exceed their established limits and as countries classified as the objects of Great Power intervention acquire the ability to strike back in turn, or to strike first. So far it is only high-explosive warheads that have actually been employed – by Iran and Iraq against each other. But chemical warheads with nerve gas fillers are seemingly ready for use, and they could inflict far higher casualties per strike in certain circumstances, against certain targets.

Nuclear warheads would, of course, place the threat in a wholly different category, so much so that the particular nature of their vehicle would lose much of its significance. There is a connection, nevertheless, and it is sinister indeed. The same transnational relationships of individuals, corporations, and state authorities that have made possible the diffusion of ballistic missile technology to scientifically backward countries such as Iraq stand ready to diffuse nuclear weapon technology also. And the same organizational techniques would be employed by the recipient: the recruitment of experts of varied national origin, their economical use in narrowly concentrated effort on nonimportable technological elements, and the purchase of adaptable civilian and "grey-area" components worldwide, in addition to acquisitions from the witting.

W. Seth Carus is the best of guides into this scarcely charted new zone of danger. He was almost the first analyst to focus on the problem and remains the most accomplished, largely because he has been willing to study patiently its technical, tactical, and industrial dimensions in all their complexities and has also made excellent use of sources otherwise quite wrongly disregarded. (Carus was the first published expert to notice that the public speeches of some Iranian leaders contained some remarkably precise technical information in addition to much theological ranting.) Very little of this apparatus shows in the text that follows, but the text is informed by it nevertheless, to the reader's signal advantage.

Finally, Carus does not fail to deduce the key political and strategic implications at each remove. He has not produced a technical work for technicians but rather an important contribution to the literature on international affairs that ought to be of considerable value for observers and practitioners alike.

Edward N. Luttwak
The Arleigh A. Burke Chair in Strategy
Center for Strategic and International Studies

About the Author

W. Seth Carus is an Olin Fellow at the Naval War College Foundation in Newport, R.I. He is currently preparing several papers on missile proliferation in the Third World. Before receiving this fellowship, Carus was a fellow at the Washington Institute for Near East Policy, where he published extensively on military affairs in the Middle East. His recent research papers include "The Genie Unleashed: Iraqi Chemical and Biological Weapons," "Chemical Weapons in the Middle East," and "Missiles in the Middle East: A New Threat to Stability?" Carus received a Ph.D. in international relations from Johns Hopkins University in 1987.

Acknowledgments

This study of missile proliferation was made possible largely because of the assistance provided by many people. Many deserve to be mentioned, but particular thanks go to Joseph S. Bermudez, Jr., Michael Eisenstadt, Geoffrey Kemp, Edward Luttwak, Gary Milhollin, Leonard Spector, and Steven Zaloga. The Washington Institute for Near East Policy and the Naval War College Foundation each provided a base for my writing of this manuscript.

Summary

The proliferation of ballistic missiles in the Third World has posed a new type of challenge to policymakers in the United States. More than 20 Third World countries either possess surface-to-surface missiles or are trying to develop or acquire them. Current trends suggest that the number of countries with missiles will increase in the 1990s and that the capabilities of the available systems will also grow. Moreover, many of these countries have made extensive use of missiles during the 1970s and 1980s.

The missiles have been acquired in many ways. Most missiles were obtained from foreign suppliers, including the Soviet Union, the United States, and China. To an increasing extent, however, Third World countries are developing their own systems. Relying on both indigenous and imported technologies, up to 14 countries have created missile development programs. As a result, the dependence of Third World countries on imported systems is declining.

The military utility of the missiles appears to be growing, driven by the expanding size of Third World inventories and the increasing accuracy and lethality of the missiles that are starting to become available. As such, the missiles potentially threaten U.S. military forces operating in the Third World, as well as U.S. allies. The dangers will grow in the coming decade as the missiles become more sophisticated.

Third World countries have developed various military responses to missile proliferation. Some countries rely on deterrence strategies, depending on threats of retaliatory strikes to prevent hostile employment of missiles. Others rely on civil defense and passive defenses, or an elaborate strike capabilities designed to destroy missile launchers. A few countries are exploring active defenses against missiles, including antitactical ballistic missile (ATBM) systems.

The United States has attempted to slow the proliferation of ballistic missiles in a variety of ways. Washington has joined with many of its allies in the Missile Technology Control Regime (MTCR), a suppliers' agreement designed to restrict exports of missiles and missile technologies to the Third World. Efforts have been made to persuade the Soviet Union, China, and other countries to abide by the provisions of the MTCR. Bilateral discussions with proliferating countries have been held, and attempts have been made to derail specific missile programs. The difficulties involved in controlling missile technology, however, will continue to pose problems for many years.

1

Surface-to-Surface Missiles in the Third World

The proliferation of surface-to-surface missiles (SSMs) in the Third World has become a serious concern for policymakers in the United States.[1] The increasing visibility given to missile proliferation accurately reflects troubling developments. Twenty-two countries in the Third World currently possess ballistic missiles or are actively attempting to acquire them. Thirteen of these countries have programs to design and build ballistic missiles, and at least 15 have operational missile forces.[2]

Six Third World countries have fired ballistic missiles at opponents. Egypt and Syria employed them against Israel in 1973. Iran and Iraq fired missiles at each other during the Gulf War from 1980 to 1988. Libya attacked the U.S. military installation on the Italian island of Lampedusa in 1986. Finally, in 1988 and 1989, the government of Afghanistan employed missiles against guerrilla forces.

Ominously, missile development programs are often linked to efforts to produce nuclear, chemical, or biological weapons. Third World countries with unconventional weapons development programs usually have ballistic missile programs as well. At least four Third World countries have

1

already deployed nuclear or chemical warheads for missiles, and the number is expected to grow considerably during the next decade.

Ballistic and Cruise Missiles

There are two main types of surface-to-surface missiles: ballistic and cruise. A ballistic missile is an unmanned, rocket-powered weapon. It is powered during the initial launch stages, but not during the descent. As a result, it follows a curved, or ballistic, trajectory once gravity takes over. Long-range ballistic missiles fly outside the atmosphere.[3] In contrast, a cruise missile is an unmanned aircraft. Although it may use a booster rocket during launch, while in flight it depends on an air-breathing engine of a type similar to those used in airplanes.

Ballistic and cruise missiles became viable weapons during World War II. The Germans employed two competing systems: the V-1 cruise missile and the V-2 ballistic missile. More than 17,000 V-1s and 3,500 V-2s were fired at cities in England and on the Continent. They inflicted considerable damage and killed nearly 12,000 civilians.[4] In contrast, the German Air Force found that it was unable to penetrate British air defenses with manned aircraft.

The ability of the missiles to penetrate highly effective air defenses led the United States and the Soviet Union to develop more capable systems. For a variety of technical reasons, most attention was given to ballistic missiles. Given available technology before the early 1970s, it was impossible to build accurate and reliable cruise missiles capable of flying long ranges; instead, it proved easier to develop ballistic missiles with intercontinental ranges. By the early 1960s, the United States and the Soviet Union possessed impressive arsenals of ballistic missiles, including systems capable of attacking cities at intercontinental ranges.

Ballistic missiles were not available to lesser powers. The technical difficulties and the costs were so great that minor powers could not build them. Nevertheless, the prestige and perceived strategic utility of ballistic missiles led a number of countries to create missile development programs in the 1950s and 1960s. The first results of these efforts appeared in the early 1970s, when France and China deployed strategic nuclear forces equipped with ballistic missiles.

Smaller, less technologically capable countries in the Third World also tried to develop ballistic missiles. In the early 1960s, Egypt and Israel embarked on competing programs to build them. Both countries depended heavily on outside support, and, in the end, the Egyptian program proved to be a complete failure. Other countries were less ambitious and concentrated instead on building an infrastructure to support missile development. During the late 1960s and the 1970s, Third World countries were content to rely on ballistic missiles acquired from the Soviet Union and the United States. The two superpowers were often willing to meet the demand, providing missiles to at least 10 countries.

By the late 1980s, the technology to develop ballistic missiles was no longer limited to the developed world. A considerable number of Third World countries had cadres of scientists, engineers, and technicians with growing expertise and experience in building and operating ballistic missile systems. They were supported by research and development facilities and production plants that could be used to design and manufacture such weapons. As a result, more than a dozen Third World countries now have ballistic missile development programs.

Motivation to Proliferate

Third World countries have powerful incentives to acquire ballistic missiles. They are prestige weapons that demonstrate the technological sophistication of the countries that own them. More important than the possession of missiles, however, is the ability to develop and produce them. Such capabilities are a confirmation of modernization because they signify that a country has access to some of the same technologies critical to the superpowers.

It would be a mistake to assume that missiles are acquired only for reasons of prestige, however. Most of the countries with ballistic missile programs have acute security problems. Ballistic missiles can perform certain strategic and military roles better than other types of weapons. Indeed, there is good reason to believe that it is the strategic and military uses of ballistic missiles that have made them so attractive to countries in the Third World.

Political and Military Considerations

The desire for ballistic missiles can arise from political or military requirements. Even if never fired, ballistic missiles confer strategic status to the countries that possess them. Thus, a country concerned about the perception of its military position may be tempted to acquire missiles even if it does not intend to use them.

Saudi Arabia acquired ballistic missiles for this reason. In early 1988, Saudi Arabia received a small number of Chinese-built DF-3A intermediate-range ballistic missiles (known to U.S. intelligence as the CSS-2). For a variety of reasons, this transaction received enormous attention. It represented the first sale of an intermediate-range ballistic missile to any Third World country. Moreover, it was the first military equipment that Saudi Arabia had ever purchased from China or any other Communist country.

Several events appear to have sparked Saudi interest in missiles. By the middle of 1985, when China agreed in principle to supply Saudi Arabia with ballistic missiles, there were at least nine countries in the Middle East with missile forces. The only countries of any importance without missiles were Jordan and Saudi Arabia. Even such small powers as South Yemen and Kuwait had missiles. Thus, Saudi

Arabia lacked a type of weapon that most other countries in the region thought necessary.[5]

Events in the Iran-Iraq War made it impossible for Saudi Arabia to ignore missiles. In March 1985, Iran began to fire Scud-B missiles, obtained from Libya, at Iraqi cities. At that point, it was clear that an important aspect of a country's military power was defined by its possession of ballistic missiles. From a political or military perspective, it was evident that no country in the region could afford to ignore missile forces. It is thus no coincidence that Saudi Arabia reached an agreement in principle to acquire the DF-3A missiles within a few months after the first Iranian use of Scud-Bs.

The military effectiveness of the missiles is dubious at best. It appears that no more than 60 missiles were acquired, a number of little strategic significance. Moreover, the DF-3A is extremely inaccurate. It has a circular error probable (CEP) of about 2,000 meters – the distance from the intended target within which half the missiles will probably land. This makes it the least accurate ballistic missile in the Middle East. Finally, the missiles rely on liquid-fueled propulsion, which requires a laborious fueling process before launch.

Further reducing the military value of the missiles was the potential effectiveness of the Saudi Arabian Air Force. Saudi Arabia had a large inventory of fighter-bombers capable of penetrating deep into hostile airspace. Equipped with sophisticated U.S. F-15 and British Tornado fighter-bombers, the Saudi Arabian Air Force could inflict considerably more damage on an opponent than could the small number of obsolete ballistic missiles.

Saudi Arabia was less interested in obtaining a militarily effective arsenal than it was in acquiring a ballistic missile system, however. Indeed, before approaching the Chinese for the DF-3A, the Saudis first asked the United States to supply Lance missiles. That the Saudis should try to acquire a missile with a 100-kilometer range, but settle for one with a range of 2,500 kilometers, suggests how little operational considerations affected their decision making.

From a Saudi point of view, the acquisition of DF-3A missiles was a resounding success. The strong U.S. reaction to the transaction served to demonstrate the strategic importance of the new Saudi missile capability. At the same time, the military ineffectiveness of the missiles ultimately defused Israeli concerns. Thus, the Saudis were able to satisfy certain critical strategic interests without creating new problems.

Strategic Deterrence

In a number of countries, ballistic missiles are considered strategic weapons that provide a deterrent against external threats. As Judge William H. Webster, director of the Central Intelligence Agency (CIA), has noted, because ballistic missiles cannot be destroyed by existing air defenses, it is likely that "the deterrent value of missiles is higher" than for manned aircraft.[6] Military forces with such strategic capability generally seek to acquire unconventional warheads for the missiles. Some Third World countries currently have nuclear and chemical warheads, and it is possible that biological agents also may be fitted to missiles in the future.

Only one Third World country currently possesses nuclear-tipped missiles, but three to five nations could have such weapons by the end of the century. Israel is believed to have activated its nuclear-armed Jericho missiles in the 1970s. India and Pakistan may intend to place nuclear warheads on the ballistic missiles that they are now developing. South Africa also is believed capable of producing nuclear devices and has a missile program as well.[7]

A number of other countries with ballistic missile programs also are suspected of having nuclear weapons development efforts, including Argentina, Brazil, Iran, Iraq, Libya, and North Korea. Some of these countries may be able to produce nuclear devices by the end of the century. The level of sophistication, however, is such that some of these countries probably lack the scientific and financial resources to build nuclear devices small enough to be fitted to ballistic missiles.

There is also concern that a trade in nuclear weapons could emerge. Libya has attempted to purchase atomic weapons on a number of occasions. Similarly, officials in the United States feared that Saudi Arabia intended to purchase nuclear devices for the DF-3A missiles provided by China.[8]

Ballistic missiles armed with chemical agents will be far more common than nuclear-armed missiles and are considerably more likely to be used. According to U.S. officials, about 20 countries have chemical weapons programs.[9] It appears that many of the countries working on chemical weapons also have ballistic missile programs, including Egypt, Iran, Iraq, Israel, Libya, North Korea, Syria, and Taiwan. Currently, only two of these countries – Syria and North Korea – are known to have chemical warheads for missiles. Syria may possess as many as three dozen warheads filled with Sarin, a nerve agent, and North Korea appears to have chemical warheads for both FROG-7 and Scud-B missiles. There is reason to believe that Iran, Iraq, and Libya also are developing chemical warheads.

In the future, biological agents may be coupled with ballistic missiles. According to U.S. officials, 10 countries are working on biological weapons.[10] This list appears to include at least eight Third World countries: Egypt, Iran, Iraq, Israel, Libya, North Korea, Syria, and Taiwan. All of these countries have ballistic missile programs.

Ballistic missiles armed with conventional high-explosive warheads can also be used as strategic weapons. Iran and Iraq employed ballistic missiles against cities between 1981 and 1988 in an effort to undermine the morale of the enemy population. According to CIA Director Webster, "Iraq's ability to hit Tehran caused a sizeable portion of the population to flee."[11] Thus, even conventionally armed ballistic missiles can have a strategic impact considerably greater than their apparent capabilities would seem to justify.

A number of countries demonstrate a clear need for strategic deterrent forces. Israel, for example, views its arsenal of Jericho ballistic missiles, armed with nuclear warheads, as a guarantee of survival. As long as Israel possesses nuclear weapons, it will be difficult for an opponent to destroy the state. The ballistic missiles are needed to ensure that the nuclear weapons can reach the intended targets, irrespective of the status of enemy defenses.

India appears to have a similar motivation in pursuing its ballistic missile program. The Indians view their main strategic adversary as China, a country that has long possessed both nuclear weapons and ballistic missiles. In contrast, India currently has no means of delivering nuclear weapons against targets deep inside China. Hence, should India ever decide to build an inventory of nuclear weapons, it will require ballistic missiles to deliver the warheads.

Syria also relies on ballistic missiles for deterrence, though it also assigns operational missions to its missile forces. By arming a small number of Scud-B missiles with chemical weapons, Syria has created a cheap deterrent that inhibits Israeli actions. The missiles provide some protection against the possible use of nuclear weapons by Israel. More plausibly, they deter conventional attacks by Israel's air force against civilian targets. (During the 1973 Arab-Israeli War, the Israelis launched destructive attacks on industrial facilities in Syria.)

During the War of the Cities fought in March and April 1988, Iranian leaders argued that the main role of their missiles was to deter Iraqi attacks on Iranian cities. According to Hojjat ol-Eslam Hashemi-Rafsanjani, then speaker of the Iranian parliament and acting commander in chief of Iranian military forces, "for us, missiles have a deterrent role." He argued that missiles cannot win a war, declaring that "no war can be stopped through missile attacks, and the military forces, particularly the infantry, decide the course of a war." He added that Iran needed to strengthen its missile forces as quickly as possible, however, "so that the very thought of an attack with missiles will be eliminated from our neighbor's mind."[12]

The development of new missiles was placed in this context. Toward the end of March 1988, the Iranians announced that they were ready to begin production of a new missile with a range of 130 kilometers. According to Hashemi-Rafsanjani, Iran wanted to produce sufficient numbers of the new missile to make possible 20 launches a day. The missiles were to be fired at Iraqi cities, including Baghdad and Kirkuk. He indicated, however, that "Iran does not wish to embark on such a course but that it has to somehow dissuade the Iraqi Government from attacking cities."[13]

Thus, it is evident that a considerable number of countries view ballistic missiles as a form of strategic deterrence. Significantly, the context varies considerably from country to country. Iran's needs differ from Syria's, which bear little resemblance to India's. Nevertheless, all these countries perceive that certain strategic requirements can be met by possession of ballistic missiles.

Military Value

There is a growing belief in the Third World that ballistic missiles are militarily effective weapons. Indeed, a significant proportion of the missiles now under development in the Third World are clearly intended for use against hostile military forces. Missiles of this type have relatively short ranges, generally 300 kilometers or less. In some instances, it is possible to employ such short-range missiles strategically, against cities. In other cases, they are mainly targeted against military forces, as when the missiles are armed with mines or antitank bomblets. Many of these weapons have ranges of less than 100 kilometers and, in some cases, are nothing more than unguided rockets.

Among the countries that are developing missiles specifically for operational roles are Brazil, Egypt, India, Iran,

Iraq, Israel, and Pakistan. Other countries, like South Korea, have indicated a need for weapons of this type. Six countries have developed long-range artillery rockets with ranges of 45 to 100 kilometers. Some of these weapons are armed with cluster munition warheads or antitank mines.

Missiles can be used for two significant military roles. They can be used to attack strategically important military targets distant from the front lines, such as air bases, equipment storage depots, command posts, air defense sites, or logistics facilities. Alternatively, missiles can be employed against hostile ground forces near the front lines, thus interdicting the movement of units approaching the front. Enemy force concentrations can be subjected to bombardment. In either situation, the missiles would be used in roles once the exclusive preserve of attack aircraft.

Ballistic missiles have several characteristics of military value. They travel at high speeds, taking only a few minutes to reach distant targets. This is especially valuable in launching surprise attacks against opponents with strategic depth because aircraft require a considerably longer period of time. Because there are now no effective defenses against missiles already launched, these forces are certain to penetrate hostile territory (barring a mechanical or guidance failure). In addition, missiles can be fired at night, when aircraft may be unable to operate effectively. New types of missiles now being developed, such as the U.S. army tactical missile system (ATACMS), may be just as cost-effective as manned aircraft, suggesting that missiles could assume certain roles near the battlefield previously assigned to air forces.

Several countries have already demonstrated that they intend to use missiles operationally. Egypt employed FROG-7 and other rockets against Israeli forces in the Sinai in the 1973 Arab-Israeli War. Afghanistan has extensively employed Scud-B missiles against guerrilla troop concentrations. More than 1,000 were fired, an average of about three a day. According to some reports, as many as six were launched at the same target at the same time.[14]

Although it is impossible to assess the effectiveness of these attacks, there is some reason to believe that the missiles compensated in part for the inability of Afghanistan's air force to operate in the presence of U.S.-supplied Stinger antiaircraft missiles.

Syria employed missiles against Israeli air bases during the opening stages of the 1973 Arab-Israeli War. Reportedly, about 25 FROG-7 rockets were fired at several air bases in northern Israel, causing some damage and disrupting Israeli air operations. Syria's missile forces retain this mission at the present time. Syria cannot rely on its air force to penetrate Israeli airspace because of the effectiveness of Israeli air defenses. As a result, missiles provide an alternative means of closing Israeli air bases and reserve mobilization sites.[15]

Other countries clearly possess missiles intended for use against operational military targets. Israel acquired Lance missiles from the United States, apparently for use against surface-to-air missile batteries. The main targets for India's Prithvi missiles will be hostile military forces.

Exploring the Issues

The proliferation of ballistic missiles is a multifaceted issue that needs to be examined from a variety of perspectives. In the chapters that follow, some of these subjects will be explored in some detail. Chapter 2 will examine the extent of the proliferation of ballistic missiles throughout the Third World. This will include a study of where missiles and missile technology are coming from. Chapter 3 will assess the military effectiveness of ballistic missiles in a Third World context. Chapter 4 will evaluate military responses by Third World countries to missile proliferation. And finally, chapter 5 will discuss initiatives taken by the United States and its allies to slow missile proliferation and will consider alternative options.

2

Proliferation of Ballistic Missiles in the Third World

Ballistic missiles are widely available in the Third World. As of early 1990, more than 20 Third World countries either have surface-to-surface missiles or are trying to develop or acquire them.[16] In Latin America, Argentina has a program, and Brazil has two competing efforts. In East Asia, North Korea is making surface-to-surface missiles, South Korea has converted surface-to-air missiles into ballistic missiles, and Indonesia appears to be acquiring the necessary technology. Taiwan has had a program, although it may no longer be active. In South Asia, both India and Pakistan have active ballistic missile programs, and Afghanistan has missiles that were acquired from the Soviet Union starting in late 1988. In sub-Saharan Africa, South Africa is developing ballistic missile technology.

The Middle East is, at present, the most dangerous area for ballistic missile proliferation. At least 10 countries in that region now have surface-to-surface missiles, and 5 of them have missile development programs. In addition, five Middle Eastern countries—Egypt, Iran, Iraq, Libya, and Syria—have employed ballistic missiles in time of war. At the present time, any country in the Middle East that aspires to be a military power possesses ballistic missiles.

Until recently, most Third World countries obtained

their missiles from foreign suppliers because few countries had manufacturing facilities. During the past few years, however, indigenous missile industries have become increasingly important. The approaches taken by different countries have varied considerably. Some countries have taken existing missiles, which were obtained from foreign sources, and modified them to extend the range or to add more lethal warheads. A few countries build copies of foreign-designed missiles, sometimes without the assistance or knowledge of the country that originally developed the missile. A growing number of countries have indigenous missile industries to design, develop, and produce ballistic missiles.

In a number of cases, countries in the Third World have used ostensibly civilian space programs to acquire the expertise required to design and build ballistic missiles. Most of the technologies required to produce sounding rockets or space launch vehicles can be used for military programs as well. Thus, countries such as Brazil, India, and Pakistan have used their space programs to build a technology base that was eventually used to design and manufacture military systems. Other countries, such as Indonesia and South Korea, appear to be following a similar path.

The Trade in Ballistic Missiles

Most ballistic missiles in the Third World were provided by foreign suppliers—still the easiest and least expensive source for obtaining ballistic missiles. Historically, the Soviet Union has been the single largest supplier of ballistic missiles, directly providing missiles to at least 10 countries. The United States has supplied missiles to three Third World countries—Israel, South Korea, and Taiwan. As a matter of policy, however, the United States has limited its exports of missiles to North Atlantic Treaty Organization (NATO) allies since the late 1970s.

The Soviet Union and the United States, however, are becoming less important as suppliers of ballistic missiles.

The Intermediate-Range Nuclear Force (INF) treaty signed by the two superpowers significantly restricts the ability of the United States and the Soviet Union to export ballistic missiles. It prohibits the two countries from possessing missiles with a range of between 500 and 5,500 kilometers. It also forbids the transfer of missiles in this category to other countries.

The treaty prevents the United States from exporting Pershing missiles and the Soviet Union from supplying SS-23, SS-12, or SS-20 missiles. Efforts have been made by Third World countries to acquire almost all of these missiles; however, the two superpowers are now limited and may only export certain short-range ballistic missiles. The Soviet Union can provide FROG-7, Scud-B, or SS-21 missiles, and the United States can export Lance, the ATACMS, or the planned Lance follow-on. Any Third World country desiring missiles with longer ranges must now depend on other sources.

As the superpowers become less important suppliers of ballistic missiles, other countries are trying to fill the void. Three Third World countries exported missiles during the 1980s: the People's Republic of China (DF-3As to Saudi Arabia), North Korea (indigenously built Scud-Bs to Iran), and Libya (Soviet-built Scud-Bs to Iran). Other countries could enter the export market in the 1990s — for example, Argentina (Condor II) and Brazil (Avibras SS-300 or the Orbita MB/EE series).

Soviet Union

The Soviet Union bears the greater part of the responsibility for spreading ballistic missiles around the world. Most ballistic missiles in the hands of Third World countries came from the Soviet Union. As the world's largest manufacturer of short-range surface-to-surface missiles, Moscow is able to provide such weapons in large quantities. It has supplied them to at least 10 client states outside the Warsaw Pact.[17] As of early 1990, the Soviet Union remains willing to export missiles, as demonstrated by the massive supply of Scud-Bs to Afghanistan.[18]

The Soviets are known to have exported FROG-7, Scud-B, and SS-21 missiles, and there have been unconfirmed reports of SS-12 Scaleboard transfers as well. The Soviet Union has supplied missiles in sufficiently large quantities to enable some recipients to retransfer missiles to other Third World countries. In addition, the Soviet transfer of substantial numbers of Scud-B missiles enabled Iraq to build large numbers of Al-Husayn missiles, which are extensively modified Scud-Bs.

Given the quantity of missiles provided by the Soviet Union to the Third World, it is not surprising that most of the surface-to-surface missiles used during conflicts in the Third World were provided by Moscow. FROG-7 and Scud-B missiles were fired by Egypt and Syria at Israel during the 1973 Arab-Israeli conflict. Iraq fired FROG-7 and Scud-B missiles at Iran, and the Iranians retaliated with Scud-B missiles (obtained from Libya and North Korea). Libya fired Soviet-supplied Scud-B missiles at the Italian island of Lampedusa in 1986.

In recent years, the Soviet Union has become concerned about the proliferation of ballistic missiles. Events in the Middle East have highlighted the potential threat to the Soviet Union from these weapons. In early 1987, before entering into the INF treaty, the Soviets decided to deny a request by the Syrians for SS-23 missiles.[19] By early 1988, there were signs that the Soviets also were restricting shipments of Scud-B missiles to Iraq.[20] The Soviet media reacted strongly to Western press reports in July 1987 that Israel had tested a version of the Jericho missile capable of reaching Soviet territory. Similarly, the Soviets were not pleased with the supply to Saudi Arabia of Chinese-made DF-3A missiles with sufficient range to hit targets in the Soviet Union.[21]

The Soviet Union also was perturbed by Iraq's conversion of Soviet-supplied Scud-Bs into Al-Husayn missiles. The modifications hurt Soviet relations with Iran. They also endangered the INF treaty by showing how the Soviets might be able to convert medium-range missiles into intermediate-range weapons.

During the Moscow Summit in June 1988, the Soviets expressed a willingness to discuss controls on the transfer of missile technology with the United States. The two countries have now held several meetings on the subject, but no concrete results appear to have emerged.

Despite indications that the Soviets are worried about the proliferation of missiles, they remain willing to export missiles in large quantities. Afghanistan received at least 900 Soviet-built Scud-B missiles in 1988 and 1989, a massive quantity by any calculation.[22] This suggests that additional deliveries might be made to other countries as well. In addition, the Soviet Union may be able to provide missiles with longer ranges than the Scud-Bs, which have a 300-kilometer range. There are indications that the Soviet Union has developed a version of the Scud-B with a range longer than 300 kilometers, and it is possible that such missiles might be exported to the Third World. In addition, the INF treaty did not force the Soviet Union to destroy the guidance systems taken from destroyed intermediate-range missiles, and the guidance packages could be retrofitted to existing Scud-B missiles to improve accuracy or could be fitted to a new missile.

United States

Although the United States has exported a large number of surface-to-surface missiles, nearly all of them have gone to NATO countries. Moreover, most of the missiles are now obsolescent and in many cases are no longer in service.[23] Most of these missiles are associated with NATO's arsenal of tactical nuclear weapons.

U.S. exports to the Third World have been considerably more limited. Israel, South Korea, and Taiwan have received surface-to-surface missiles from the United States. South Korea and Taiwan were given MGR-1 Honest John ballistic missiles, but only South Korea retains them in inventory. South Korea was provided with 12 launchers. The last sale by the United States of ballistic missiles to the Third World took place in the mid-1970s and involved the supply of Lance missiles to Israel. It appears that the Israelis were sold 12 Lance missile launchers and at least 200 missiles, all armed with cluster munition warheads.

The United States no longer exports ballistic missiles to the Third World. Since the late 1970s, the United States has rejected requests from the Third World for ballistic missiles. An effort by Israel to obtain the Pershing 1A missile was rejected. Similarly, an attempt by Saudi Arabia to obtain Lance surface-to-surface missiles in the mid-1980s was refused.

Other Suppliers

Until the late 1980s, the supply of ballistic missiles was almost totally a monopoly of the two superpowers. The only exception took place in 1968, when France delivered a batch of MD-660 missiles to Israel. These missiles were being developed in France for the Israelis and later became the basis of the Jericho missile.

By the mid-1980s, however, the superpowers began losing control over the market in ballistic missiles. A trade in Soviet-supplied missiles began to emerge. Although the quantities involved in such transactions were small, the strategic impact of these transfers was considerable. Iran's missile forces were made possible by supplies of Scud-B missiles from Libya and North Korea. Libya is believed to have provided the Iranians with at least 30 Soviet-built and supplied Scud-B missiles in late 1984 or early 1985. By early 1988, North Korea had shipped about 100 ballistic missiles to Iran to fulfill an order placed two years before.[24]

The People's Republic of China entered the picture as a supplier in 1988, when it delivered DF-3A intermediate-range ballistic missiles to Saudi Arabia. Although China initiated development of ballistic missiles in the early 1960s, it was not until the contract with Saudi Arabia that China emerged as an exporter of such weapons. By 1988, China was actively promoting the sale of a new generation of more advanced M-9 and M-11 missiles to countries throughout the Middle East.[25] U.S. diplomacy appears to have convinced China of the potential dangers of selling such missiles. As a result, it appears that China is no longer overtly marketing its M-series missiles.[26]

In the future, several other countries may be in a position to act as suppliers of ballistic missiles. The most likely candidates are Argentina and Brazil. Argentina is developing the Condor II missile, and Brazil has two known missile programs in the works. All these programs are intended for export. The economic incentive to export missiles is strong. Argentina, Brazil, China, Egypt, and North Korea all appear to be in a position to earn substantial revenues through sales of missiles or missile components. Argentina is reported to have received several hundred million dollars for development of the Condor II missile, and China may have received as much as $3 billion for the DF-3 missiles sold to Saudi Arabia. Libya was supposed to give Brazil as much as $2 billion over a five-year period to support development of the Orbita MB/EE family of missiles. The North Koreans may have received several hundred million dollars from the Iranians to pay for Scud-B missiles.

Indigenous Development and Production

Numerous Third World countries are trying to design and build missiles without having to buy completed systems from the industrialized world. CIA Director William Webster has suggested that 15 countries in the Third World may be producing ballistic missiles by the year 2000.[27] Although there is reason to doubt that so many countries will be making ballistic missiles in a decade, clearly numerous missile programs are now in development.

A variety of approaches have been adopted by countries seeking to build missiles. Several countries are content to modify versions of existing missiles extensively, while others produce copies of foreign designs. A growing number of countries, however, are trying to produce missiles of indigenous design.

Missile Modification

A number of countries are believed to have made surface-to-surface missiles by modifying surface-to-air missiles obtained from foreign sources. In 1978, South Korea tested a modified version of the U.S. Nike Hercules surface-to-air missile with a surface-to-surface capability.[28]

The most successful missile modification program was launched by Iraq. Between 1985 and 1988, the Iraqis were able to convert existing inventories of Scud-B missiles, which had a range of only 300 kilometers, into Al-Husayn (range of 650 kilometers) and Al-Abbas (range of 900 kilometers) missiles. The first reported launch of the Al-Husayn took place in August 1987, but Iraq had enough of these missiles in inventory to fire about 190 of them at Iranian cities in early 1988. According to Iranian assessments, the Al-Husayn was produced by cannibalizing one Scud-B missile to provide inserts to increase the size of the fuel and oxidizer tanks on two other Scud-B missiles. This added about 1.3 meters to the length of the missile and increased the amount of propellent by about 25 percent. In April 1988, the Iraqis announced a successful test launch of the Al-Abbas, also based on Scud-B technology.

Copying Foreign Designs

Several countries manufacture missiles copied from foreign-developed systems. North Korea is now building its own version of the Scud-B, and Iran has attempted to do the same. Egypt is believed to have mounted a similar effort to copy the Scud-B, but it is not known if it ever entered production. In 1981, Taiwan displayed the Ching Feng, a surface-to-surface missile that looked suspiciously like the U.S. Lance.[29]

Indigenous Designs

Several countries in the Third World now produce locally developed missiles. Two countries, Iran and Israel, are believed to have placed in service indigenously designed missiles. At least 10 other countries are believed to have active missile development programs, including Argentina, Brazil, Egypt, India, Indonesia, Iraq, Libya, North Korea, Pakistan, South Korea, and Taiwan.

The Israelis have the most sophisticated program. The latest version of their Jericho missile is believed to have a range of 1,500 kilometers. According to experts who have analyzed the performance of their Shavit satellite launch vehicle, the Israelis appear to have the technology required to build an intercontinental ballistic missile (ICBM) with a range in excess of 5,000 kilometers.[30]

Iran has an extremely active missile development effort. Relying heavily on assistance from China, the Iranians have fielded several different short and medium-range missiles. They have a number of short-range unguided rockets, including the 45-kilometer Oghab, the Shahin-2, and the Nazeat. In addition, they claim to have tested missiles with ranges of 120 kilometers, 160 kilometers, and 200 kilometers. It is believed that some of the longer-range missiles may be entering production.[31]

Both India and Pakistan have missile programs. India has successfully tested two separate programs: the Prithvi with a 250-kilometer range and the Agni with a 2,500-kilometer range. The Prithvi was tested in 1988 and the Agni in 1989. Press reports suggest that India is also working on a missile with a range of 5,000 kilometers. It is generally agreed that the Indian military missile program was a beneficiary of technology provided by Western countries for use by India's civilian space program.[32] Pakistan has the

Hatf-1 and Hatf-2 missiles under development. The Hatf-1 has a range of 80 kilometers and the Hatf-2 a range of 300 kilometers.

Brazil has been developing two different ballistic missiles under the auspices of competing companies. The SS-300 is being developed by Avibras, the firm that built the 60-kilometer Astros II artillery rockets provided to a number of countries in the Middle East. Additional versions of the SS-300 with ranges of 600 and 1,000 kilometers are also planned.[33] Recent reports suggest that development of the SS-300 may have been held up by a lack of funding and by a lack of government support. The SS-300 has been shown to the Iraqis and the Libyans, but there is no evidence that either country has agreed to fund development of the SS-300.[34]

Orbita is currently developing the MB/EE family of surface-to-surface missiles. This missile is based on the technology employed in the Sonda IV sounding rocket developed by Brazil's space program. The first version to be produced is the MB/EE-150, which will have a range of between 100 and 150 kilometers and will carry a 500-kilogram warhead. Other versions of the missile will have ranges of 300, 600, and 1,000 kilometers.[35]

Technology Transfer

Foreign assistance plays an important role in the development of missile forces in the Third World. Most countries in the Third World lack the scientific and engineering resources to develop ballistic missiles on their own. As a result, they are forced to search for foreign sources of components or technical expertise.

In a few cases, countries have found it possible to avoid active assistance from outside sources by copying existing missiles. In most cases, this means copying relatively old technology. The North Korean, Iraqi, and Egyptian programs all rely to varying degrees on Scud-B technology. In such cases, the countries involved are taking advantage of a

fairly old and well-understood technology because the
Scud-B is essentially an updated German V-2 of World War
II origin. The more sophisticated programs, however, require considerable assistance from the industrialized world.
It is thus not surprising that West European scientists and
engineers are actively working on such programs throughout the Third World.

West Germans have provided assistance to missile programs in Argentina, Brazil, Egypt, India, Iraq, and Libya.
Although the Federal Republic of Germany has never built
a ballistic missile for its own use, West German engineers
remain familiar with state-of-the-art technology. During the
1980s, a leading West German defense contractor, Mes-
serschmitt-Boelkow-Blohm (known as MBB) designed the
Kolas missile, a conventionally armed ballistic missile designed for attacks on air bases and other critical targets. It
appears that MBB worked closely with a U.S. company,
Martin Marietta, which was responsible for building the
Pershing II intermediate-range ballistic missile. As a result,
MBB seems to have been intimately familiar with the most
advanced U.S. missile technology.[36]

The most widely reported project involving the partici-
pation of West German companies and individuals is the
Condor II. The Condor II originated in Argentina and is
scheduled to have a range of 800 kilometers. The U.S. government believes that MBB has actively assisted the Argen-
tineans and Egyptians in the development of the missile. In
addition, another German defense company, MAN, was responsible for building the mobile launchers for the Condor.[37]
A subsidiary of MBB, Transtechnica, is believed to provide
technical support for the Egyptian missile program.[38]

It is possible to discover similar kinds of activity elsewhere. A number of West German countries are helping
Iraq to put together the Saad 16 complex in northern Iraq.
Press reports suggest that Iraq is spending more than $200
million to build this facility, which will provide the capabilities to develop many different types of missiles, including
ballistic and cruise.

The ongoing Libyan program started with the activity of Otrag, a West German company, and has continued since then with the presence of German engineers hired directly by the Libyan government. West German scientists are also involved in the development of India's space launch vehicle.[39]

The Chinese have become an important supplier of ballistic missile technology to Third World countries. Brazil has sought to overcome technical flaws in the design of its space launch vehicle by acquiring liquid fuel rocket technology from China.[40] Press reports suggest that Iran's missile program has obtained considerable amounts of technical assistance from China.[41] Moreover, China may have provided the North Koreans with critical components for the Scud-B missiles made in North Korea and exported to Iran.[42] The Pakistani missile program also probably relies to some extent on Chinese technology.[43]

France provides technology to several programs, helping, for example, Argentina, Egypt, and India. A French company, SNPE, cooperated with Egypt in the design of the Sakr-80 missile and was primarily responsible for the solid fuel rocket motor.[44] European press reports also suggest that the guidance package for the Condor II missile was provided by SAGEM, another French aerospace company.[45] French companies are believed to be providing the strap-on booster rockets that India uses for its advanced space launch vehicle (ASLV).

An Italian company, SNIA-BPD, is reported to have participated in the Condor program. SNIA-BPD has considerable expertise in rocket technology and is responsible for making the solid fuel booster rockets used on the European Ariane space launch vehicles. Italian press reports suggest that a group of SNIA-BPD engineers created a number of front companies to provide support for the Condor. It appears that some of the transactions may have violated Italian export laws.[46]

In addition, Third World countries are starting to cooperate in the development of missiles, transferring technolo-

gy from one Third World country to another. Egypt may
have provided samples of the Scud-B missile that enabled
the North Koreans to initiate their development program.[47]
It is generally believed that the Iraqi Al-Husayn and Al-
Abbas missiles were built with assistance from Egypt. Currently, Iraq is negotiating possible joint missile development with Brazilian companies. The South African ballistic
missile program is believed to be based on technology provided by Israel. Other reports have suggested that Israel
may have assisted both China and Taiwan to develop surface-to-surface missiles.[48]

The Role of "Civilian" Space Programs

A number of countries in the Third World have space
programs intended to produce rockets capable of placing
satellites into space. At present, only two Third World
countries, India and Israel, have orbited a satellite. At least
eight other countries, however—Argentina, Brazil, Indonesia, Iraq, Pakistan, South Africa, South Korea, and Taiwan—have civilian space programs for the ostensible pur-
pose of building satellite launch vehicles.

In reality, there is reason to doubt that a distinction can
be made between a purely civilian space program and a
military program. Six of the seven countries that have
placed satellites into orbit also produce military ballistic
missiles.[49] The Israeli space program provides a vivid illus-
tration of the close relationship between military missiles
and civilian satellite launch vehicles. The Israeli Shavit satellite launch vehicle, used in September 1988 to place a
satellite into orbit, is believed to be a version of the Jericho
surface-to-surface missile. The relation between civilian and
military rocket programs is particularly clear in those Third
World countries with the most advanced space institutes.

When South Africa announced that it had successfully
tested a "rocket booster" in July 1989, for example, it was

Armscor – a government-owned armaments manufacturer – that released the information.[50] Moreover, the South African press noted that the government intended the space
program for "communication, commercial, industrial, and
military purposes."[51] It is difficult to imagine that any technology developed for putting satellites in orbit could not be
used to develop surface-to-surface missiles as well.

The Brazilian space program has developed several
Sonda sounding rockets. These rockets have been adapted
for use as artillery rockets with ranges up to 68 kilometers,
and they have been exported to the Middle East. It is believed that this same technology will be the basis for future
Brazilian surface-to-surface missiles as well.

Links between the Indian civilian and military rocket
programs are equally clear. The technical director of the
Indian Prithvi project formerly headed the Indian effort to
develop the SLV-3 rocket, which was used to put India's
first satellite into space. The Agni intermediate-range ballistic missile is the first stage of the SLV-3 rocket.[52]

Pakistan is another country that has a civilian space
program linked to a military missile program. The Space
and Upper Atmosphere Research Committee (SUPARCO)
is responsible for the development of missiles in Pakistan.
This organization is directly controlled by a Supreme Space
Research Council chaired by the president of Pakistan.[53]
Publicly, SUPARCO is involved solely in exploiting space
for civilian purposes, but it is generally believed that it is
also responsible for developing missile systems for military
purposes. SUPARCO manufactures solid fuel rocket motors and the propellants used in them.[54]

Pakistani sources indicate that they are on the verge of
launching a satellite into space. A statement released in
January 1988 anticipated that the Badr experimental satellite would be placed in orbit in June. The satellite weighs 75
kilograms and will be placed in an orbit of 300 to 400 kilometers. The satellite was produced entirely by Pakistani
personnel, but "with the assistance and cooperation of Arab

countries."[55] The launch had not taken place by early 1990, suggesting that technical problems were delaying the program.

Future Developments

Ballistic missiles are now widely available in the Third World. The countries that possess missiles remain dependent on a small number of potential suppliers, especially the Soviet Union. This dependence is beginning to end, however, and several countries are now able to manufacture missiles without overt assistance from abroad. Moreover, as the number of missiles in the Third World increases, the likelihood of third party transfers have also increased.

By the early 1990s, several countries in the Third World are likely to manufacture missiles in relatively large numbers, and several of them will be willing to export those missiles. Among the countries that may be able to produce missiles will be Argentina, Brazil, Egypt, India, Iran, Iraq, Israel, North Korea, Pakistan, South Korea, and Taiwan. Several of these producers will probably be willing to export missiles to other Third World countries.

Thus, the number of countries possessing ballistic missiles is likely to increase in the next few years, and dependence on non–Third World suppliers is likely to diminish. By the mid-1990s, it is likely that the Soviet Union and the United States will largely have lost control of the market in ballistic missiles.

3

Capabilities of Ballistic Missiles

Ballistic missiles possess unique capabilities that make them potentially useful as conventional military weapons. First, they are capable of traveling long distances in relatively short periods of time. Second, existing air defenses are unable to intercept ballistic missiles, so that missiles are assured of penetrating the intended target. Third, it may be easier for a country to operate a missile force than an air force. In some cases, ballistic missiles might be the only practical means of attacking targets at long ranges.

Speed of Attack

Ballistic missiles can deliver payloads over long distances in short periods of time. A ballistic missile with a maximum range of 900 kilometers requires only nine minutes to fly the entire distance. Short-range ballistic missiles take even less time. The Soviet-made SS-21, with a range of 100 kilometers, takes only three to four minutes to reach its maximum range.[56] By contrast, a strike aircraft can fly at a speed greater than 1,000 kilometers per hour, taking nearly an hour to fly 900 kilometers. It would take no more than six minutes to cover 100 kilometers.

A practical example of the difference between aircraft

and ballistic missiles is given by the Iraqi experience in the Gulf War. In early 1987, Iraq used its Mirage F-1 fighter-bombers to bomb Tehran.[57] The aircraft had to travel about 650 kilometers from air bases to the Iranian capital. It probably took the planes about 45 minutes to reach the city. In contrast, the Iraqi Al-Husayn missiles required only seven to eight minutes to cover the same distance.

There are obvious circumstances when this speed may be of critical military importance. Aircraft may take too long to reach targets deep in enemy territory during the opening stages of a surprise attack. Thus, if Syria were to attack Israel, it might take strike aircraft as long as 30 minutes to reach air bases in southern Israel. By the time the attacking aircraft reached their targets, the air bases would likely have been alerted. As a result, the defenders would be ready for the attack, and a significant number of defending aircraft would have been launched. By contrast, a ballistic missile would have taken only five minutes to cover the same distance.

Assured Penetration

There is no existing method of destroying ballistic missiles after they have been launched because the missiles travel too fast for conventional antiaircraft defenses to shoot them down. Every missile fired will reach its target, barring mechanical failure of some kind. This assured penetration provides ballistic missiles a significant military advantage over manned aircraft.

The increasing quality of air defense has made the invulnerability of missiles particularly important. The effectiveness of air defense can vary considerably, depending both on the quality of the antiaircraft weaponry and on the ability of attacking aircraft to suppress any defense. A modern, well-run air defense system might shoot down 1 to 4 percent of all aircraft entering defended airspace.

Even most Third World countries now possess sophisticated air defense systems capable of detecting, intercepting, and destroying strike aircraft. Typically, these systems are provided with elaborate command and control systems, surveillance radar, interceptor aircraft, surface-to-air missile batteries, and antiaircraft artillery.

The increased capabilities of air defenses in the Third World, the growing cost of acquiring and maintaining air forces, and the difficulties of operating modern fighter aircraft have all made ballistic missiles increasingly attractive. As a result, it is possible that some countries may find a missile force to be more useful militarily than an air force.

Although air defense systems have not made manned aircraft obsolete or ineffective, they have made it more difficult and expensive to employ air power. The presence of air defense systems requires the use of highly sophisticated strike aircraft. High performance engines are needed to move the plane through enemy airspace as quickly as possible, shortening its exposure to enemy air defenses. Sophisticated navigation and attack systems are needed, including high quality radar, to allow a pilot to locate and designate the intended target at distances beyond the reach of antiaircraft weapons. The aircraft must be equipped to operate stand-off munitions that can be released at long ranges. Finally, they must be equipped with sophisticated self-protection systems, including warning devices to detect enemy air defense radar and missiles and electronic countermeasures to defeat radar-guided and infrared homing guns and missiles.

To combat effective air defenses, an air force has to conduct a significant number of sorties against them. Although such tactics might reduce the effectiveness of air defenses, every aircraft used in this way cannot be used against other targets. In addition, ground attack sorties are conducted so as to minimize exposure to air defenses, which lessens effectiveness. As a result, aircraft make less accurate deliveries and cause less damage to ground targets than would otherwise have been the case.

The difficulties posed by air defenses are evident when one examines the contrasting difficulties that face the Israeli and Syrian air forces. The Syrian Air Force has an inventory of about 650 combat aircraft, including some of the most modern fighters exported by the Soviet Union — the MiG-29s, MiG-25s, and MiG-23s. Moreover, it is believed that Su-24 Fencer long-range strike aircraft are on order. Syrian planes are equipped with sophisticated laser-guided air-to-ground missiles.[58] By any measure, Syria's air force has impressive capabilities.

Nevertheless, Syria cannot rely on its air force should a war break out with Israel. It is generally recognized that Syrian aircraft would have considerable difficulty penetrating any distance into Israeli airspace. Although Israel has only a small number of surface-to-air missile batteries and antiaircraft guns, it has demonstrated considerable effectiveness in the use of fighters to intercept and shoot down enemy aircraft. The results of the 1982 Lebanon War indicate the extent of the problem facing the Syrians. According to one set of statistics, the Syrian Air Force lost 82 fighters during only 266 sorties, giving it a loss rate of about 30 percent.[59] Thus, the Syrians lost 30 of every 100 fighters that they sent into Lebanon. If these loss rates were suffered during a larger war, a typical Syrian aircraft would survive on average to make only 2.25 missions, and the entire Syrian Air Force would disappear after only seven days. Accordingly, it is not surprising that Syria has devoted considerable effort to developing its ballistic missile forces.

The Iran-Iraq War reinforces this point. Iran was unable to acquire manned combat aircraft during the hostilities, but it was able to obtain quantities of ballistic missiles. Moreover, its Scud-B missiles were operated by the Islamic Revolution Guards Corps (IRGC), a force not known for its technical expertise.

Disadvantages

Despite the operational advantages of missiles, they also possess a number of technical weaknesses. Two factors reduce the military usefulness of ballistic missiles under current circumstances. First, most existing ballistic missiles in the Third World are older types that are ineffective against point military targets – for example, the Soviet Scud-Bs and the Chinese DF-3s. Even more modern missiles suffer from similar problems, however: Neither the Chinese M-9 missile nor the Condor II is particularly accurate. Until missiles begin to appear that are considerably more accurate and substantially more lethal, ballistic missiles will be used mainly as terror weapons to attack urban concentrations.

Second, ballistic missiles are used for missions that often can be assigned to a manned strike aircraft. A well-trained air force, appropriately equipped with electronic warfare systems, command and control systems, advanced munitions, and sophisticated aircraft, remains formidable, despite improvements in air defense.

Surface-to-surface missiles are used mainly to deliver ordnance against ground targets, a role that aircraft could probably fill at least as well. Indeed, in many respects, aircraft are probably superior to missiles. Unlike ballistic missiles, which can be used only once, aircraft are reusable. They also are more adaptable. Aircraft can be assigned to a wide variety of missions largely because they can carry a diverse array of ordnance. They can assess battle damage immediately after attacking a target; ballistic missiles have no way of providing such information. Finally, a manned aircraft carries a pilot who can react to changing circumstances.

Military Effectiveness

The military effectiveness of ballistic missiles depends on technical and operational characteristics. Obviously important are range, accuracy, and warhead type, but equally significant are the rates of fire that can be sustained.

Range

The majority of the ballistic missiles now in the Third World have relatively short ranges. The missile most commonly available is the Scud-B, which has a range of only

300 kilometers. Many of the other missiles, such as the Lance, the SS-21, or the FROG-7, have even shorter ranges. Ranges have begun to lengthen, however. At least three countries operate missiles with ranges of more than 300 kilometers. Iraq has Al-Abbas missiles with a range of 900 kilometers and Al-Husayn missiles with a range of 650 kilometers. Israel has Jericho missiles with a range of 1,500 kilometers. Saudi Arabia has DF-3A missiles with a range of 2,500 kilometers. India has successfully test-fired the Agni, which is reported to have a range of 2,500 kilometers. Other countries known to be interested in developing missiles with such long ranges include Argentina, Brazil, Libya, and South Korea.

Although greater range does not make a missile more destructive, it does increase the extent of the area that can be hit. A long range also can enhance operational flexibility. A missile with short range that has to be fired from launch sites in forward positions is vulnerable to enemy counterstrikes. A missile with a longer range can be fired from deep in friendly territory, complicating the enemy's task of locating the missile launchers.

In many circumstances, however, even short-range ballistic missiles can be militarily useful. Almost every militarily significant target in Iraq is within 300 kilometers of Iran. Thus, Iran does not need long-range missiles to strike Iraq. Similarly, nearly all strategic locations in Israel are within 350 kilometers of Syrian territory, and most potential targets are within 150 kilometers. Neither Syria nor Iran necessarily requires missiles with intermediate ranges, but can do quite well with short-range systems.

Missile Accuracy

The importance of accuracy in assessing the effectiveness of a ballistic missile depends on the character of the intended target and the nature of the missile's warhead. Accuracy may not matter very much in the attack of area targets — military installations spread over large areas (such as equipment storage sites) or heavily populated urban centers. If it is possible to fire large numbers of missiles at the same target, reduced accuracy can be acceptable. A nuclear-armed missile can be relatively inaccurate if fired at a large city; missing the aim point by 1,000 or even 2,000 meters will make little difference in the destructive effects of the atomic blast. Similarly, a missile with a chemical weapons payload fired at an area target, such as a city or equipment storage depot, may not need to be very accurate.

In many circumstances, however, accuracy is critical. True accuracy is especially important when employing conventionally armed missiles against point targets, such as surface-to-air missile sites, air bases, or radar installations.

Most of the missiles currently available to Third World countries incorporate 1950s and 1960s guidance technology and are extremely inaccurate. The most common surface-to-surface missile in the Third World is the Soviet-designed Scud-B, which has a CEP of about 1,000 meters. Thus, the CEP equals about 0.3 percent of the maximum range of 300 kilometers. The accuracy of the U.S. Lance missile appears to be roughly comparable: a CEP of between 150 and 400 meters and a range of 110 kilometers, or between 0.15 percent and 0.4 percent of range.[60] By comparison, modern fighters are fitted with sophisticated weapon delivery systems that make it possible for them to drop conventional, unguided high explosive bombs within 5 to 15 meters of the intended target. Precision-guided weapons can be delivered with even greater accuracy.

Many of the new missiles now being developed for use in the Third World are no more accurate than older systems. The Chinese advertised that the M-9 missile will be accurate to about 0.1 percent of range, suggesting a CEP of about 650 meters. The Condor II missile will have a similar accuracy—that is, a CEP of about 800 meters. Given the extended range of these two missiles, they demonstrate improved accuracy beyond the existing generation of missiles available to Third World countries. But they are still capable only of attacking area targets, which makes them suitable mainly for terrorist strikes against civilian areas, unless they are armed with chemical or nuclear warheads.

It is only a matter of time before military forces in the Third World begin to replace their existing inaccurate inventories of missiles with newer, more accurate systems. The possibilities are evident from examining Soviet missiles introduced in the early 1980s. During that period, a new generation of missiles was adopted to replace the FROG-7, the Scud-B, and the SS-12 Scaleboard missiles fielded in the 1960s and 1970s. The FROG-7 had a CEP of 400 meters and is being replaced by the SS-21 with a CEP of 240 to 300 meters. The Scud-B was in the process of being replaced by the SS-23, which has a CEP of 320 to 350 meters. The Soviet SS-12 Scaleboard also was improved. The old missile had a CEP of 650 meters (or even more), compared with a CEP of only 300 meters for the new SS-12M version of the system.[61]

As countries in the Third World develop a new generation of guidance systems, comparable to those introduced a decade ago by the Soviet Union, the accuracy of their missiles should improve considerably. Even with accuracies of this type, however, the missiles will not be able to strike point targets unless armed with an area attack warhead.

Warhead

The destructiveness of a missile depends in part on the warhead that it carries. Most missiles are fitted with relatively small warheads that usually weigh between 500 and 1,000 kilograms — a fraction of the payload typically carried by modern attack aircraft. Fighter-bombers such as the F-4 Phantom or the F-16 can carry as much as 8,000 kilograms of ordnance (although normally they will carry no more than 2,000 to 4,000 kilograms) even over long ranges. Each of the Israeli F-16s that attacked the Iraqi nuclear reactor at Osiraq carried two bombs weighing about 1,000 kilograms each.[62]

Thus, delivery of the same ordnance carried by a single

aircraft can require a large number of missiles. The payload of a single F-16 is equal to that of four Scud-B missiles. It would take 10 Iraqi Al-Husayn missiles (with warheads of only about 190 kilograms each of explosives) to equal the payload carried by a single F-16.

Under certain circumstances, however, it is not possible to measure the destructiveness of tactical ballistic missiles in such simple ways. Supersonic speeds impart considerable energy to ballistic missiles when they land, especially when the missile does not separate from the warhead or separates just before impact. The Scud-B travels at three times the speed of sound when it lands, not only exploding unexpended fuel but causing considerable damage with the impact of its two-ton missile fuselage. German tests of the V-2 rocket, which is a predecessor of the Soviet Scud missile, revealed that even without a warhead, the missile could create a crater 30 to 40 meters in diameter and 10 to 15 meters deep.

This destructive capability is confirmed by experience with missiles during the Iran-Iraq War. Missiles fired at Baghdad and Tehran have caused tremendous damage, seemingly out of proportion to the size of the warhead. In some cases, entire streets of shops and houses were destroyed. In other instances, reinforced concrete skyscrapers were devastated by missile strikes. Typically, the missiles left craters at least 10 meters across and several meters deep.[63]

It is possible to enhance the lethality of missiles by using more potent warheads. Most existing missiles are armed with conventional high explosive warheads. These are usually unitary warheads that consist of a large explosive charge weighing between 500 and 1,000 kilograms. New missiles will incorporate modern submunitions, a trend that will accelerate in the next few years.

Typical of the new generation of missiles is Egypt's Sakr-80 rocket. This missile will be fitted with three different warheads: a cluster bomb warhead with 950 bomblets, a mine warhead with 65 antitank minelets, and an anti-armored warhead with high explosives imbedded with spherical balls capable of penetrating light armor plating.[64] Similarly, the Iraqis have developed versions of their Ababil 50 and 100-kilometer range rockets fitted with cluster munitions and mines, and they claim to have a cluster munition warhead for their FROG-7 rockets.[65]

Indian sources indicate that their Prithvi missile will be capable of carrying a payload of as much as 1,000 kilograms with a range of about 250 kilometers. Five conventional payloads are reportedly under development, including a high explosive warhead, three cluster munitions warheads (filled with armor-piercing bomblets, incendiary bomblets, or bomblets), and a secret warhead known as "BCES," possibly a fuel air explosive.[66]

Rates of Fire

The effectiveness of missile attacks also depends on the number of missiles that can be fired. Even if individual missiles can inflict considerable damage, only the collective impact of a large number of missiles can influence the course of a war.

Although a large number of missiles were fired during the course of the Iran-Iraq War, neither country was able to fire large quantities in a short period of time. The Iraqis never fired more than 11 missiles in one day, and they never fired more than 7 missiles during any 12-hour period. During the 1973 Arab-Israeli War, the Syrians were able to fire no more than 7 missiles in one day. There is good reason to believe that, during a short war, it would be impossible for any country to fire large numbers of missiles.

The same limitations are likely to restrict the effectiveness of other missiles in the Third World. The DF-3A missiles supplied by China to Saudi Arabia are unlikely to be much improved over other 1960s vintage missiles. Firing these missiles is likely to be a slow process, because of lengthy preparation time and the limited number of available launchers. Only the arrival of new generation missiles that can be treated as "wooden" rounds (weapons that can be used out of the container with minimal preparation) and designed for rapid fire will eliminate this bottleneck. Missiles of the future will be capable of rapid fire, because they will require less preparation time and will be easier to transport and handle. Possible changes are suggested by experience with short-range missiles. The Iranians claim that they have been able to fire as many as 32 Oghab rockets in a single day.

The impact of limited inventories and slow rates of fire is evident in the experience of the Iraqi air and missile forces during the 1988 War of the Cities. Between February 29 and March 14, 1988, the Iraqis indicate that they fired 68 Al-Husayn missiles at Iranian cities. The weight of the explosives carried by the Al-Husayns amounted to less than 13 tons, although this significantly understates the net destructive effect of the missiles. During that same period, the Iraqi Air Force was able to drop 731 bombs weighing just under 314 tons on Iranian cities.[67] Even if it is assumed that the net destructive effect of an Al-Husayn missile was the equivalent of 2 tons of bombs, the Iraqi Air Force was still able to deliver two-and-a-half times more ordnance than the missile force.

At the same time, the Iran-Iraq War has demonstrated that countries can readily obtain large supplies of missiles and that they can readily replace expended inventories. At the start of the war in 1980, Iraq is reported to have possessed only 12 Scud-B launchers and probably had no more than 100 missiles. Iran had no Scud missiles. Yet, during Iran-Iraq War, more than 400 Scud-type missiles were fired by the two countries, at least 300 by Iraq and more than 110 by Iran.[68]

The potential availability of missiles was further demonstrated by the quantity of Scud-B missiles fired by the Afghan government in late 1988 and early 1989. Reports suggest that more than 500 missiles were fired in a six-month period and that often as many as six were launched at the same time at the same target. The total cost of the missiles was estimated by U.S. sources at about $500 million or $1 million per missile.[69]

New Generation Tactical Ballistic Missiles

The tactical ballistic missiles that have been used in combat since World War II have been older generation Soviet weapons—the Scud-B and FROG-7. They are considerably less dangerous than the newer tactical ballistic missiles now entering service. The state-of-the-art is demonstrated by a new conventionally armed tactical ballistic missile, the ATACMS, being developed in the United States. Despite its 150-kilometer range, it will be fired from the same launcher vehicle used with the 30-kilometer range multiple-launched rocket system (MLRS) artillery rocket. The ATACMS will be stored, transported, and fired from a container, minimizing the difficulties of handling and preparing it for launch. It will carry a payload 70 percent larger than that of the older Lance missile. Moreover, it will be three times more accurate. Initially, the ATACMS will carry a cluster-bomb warhead, but eventually the missiles will be armed with terminally guided munitions. All of this will be obtained in a system costing only $400,000.[70]

If it is possible to manufacture ballistic missiles at the cost of the ATACMS, the operational role of the ballistic missile will be altered in a fundamental way. No longer will the ballistic missile merely be a specialized piece of equipment, suitable only for esoteric missions. Armed with conventional weapons, ballistic missiles can be a critical component of a coordinated first strike intended to cripple enemy military forces in the opening stages of a conflict.

Commentators in the Third World suggest that it will be possible to build long-range missiles with high accuracy in the 1990s. They indicate that a state-of-the-art missile with a range of 1,000 kilometers could have a CEP of no more than 50 meters.[71] This implies a missile with an accuracy of 0.005 percent of range, or about 5 meters for every 100 kilometers of range. These capabilities are quite impressive, comparable to those achieved by the United States with its Pershing II missile, which had a CEP of only 40 meters, compared with 400 meters for the older Pershing 1A.[72]

Experts in the United States are skeptical of claims of this type. They note that the difficulties involved in producing highly accurate ballistic missiles are great. Moreover, the Pershing II relies on a highly sophisticated terrain comparison system (TERCOM) that uses radar to map the target area, compares the resulting map with one stored in memory, and adjusts the trajectory of the reentry vehicle to compensate for aiming errors. Currently, the United States is the only country known to have fielded such systems. Nevertheless, it should be noted that engineers in the Third World believe that they can develop missiles with high accuracy, suggesting they believe they can gain access to comparable technologies.

It is the cruise missile, however, that will pose the most serious challenges in the 1990s. The technologies required to build conventionally armed cruise missiles will be within the reach of a considerable number of countries in the Third World.

Cruise missile guidance systems will be readily available, especially as commercial applications of the Global Positioning System (GPS) become widespread. GPS systems make use of navigational signals transmitted by satellites. The use of GPS receivers costing only a few thousand dollars make it possible for cruise missiles to achieve accuracies of less than 100 meters, even at long ranges. Moreover, by taking advantage of the inexpensive technologies being developed for remotely piloted vehicles and drones, it should be possible to build those missiles at relatively low costs. Tied together with cluster munitions, intelligent submunitions, and fuel air explosives, cruise missiles will have the accuracy and lethality to be extraordinarily effective.

4

Third World Military Responses to Ballistic Missiles

Military forces in the Third World have responded to the threats posed by ballistic missiles in a variety of ways. Countermeasures have included the following:

- destruction of missile launchers
- threatened or actual retaliatory attacks against enemy economic and political targets
- hardening of critical military installations
- comprehensive civil defense protection for the entire civilian population
- electronic countermeasures
- development of antitactical ballistic missile systems.

The responses adopted vary from one country to another, depending on military, political, economic, and geographic circumstances.

The nature of the threat is a central consideration. If missiles are seen to pose only a limited danger, there tends to be little willingness to invest in potentially costly countermeasures. In contrast, when the threat is severe, an intense search for countermeasures will result.

The selection of particular options from the range of

potential countermeasures depends on strategic and doctrinal considerations, technological capabilities, and organizational imperatives. The character of the potential targets will dictate in part the nature of the response. Missiles directed against population centers must be handled differently from those fired at military installations. It may be possible to deter attacks on urban areas by retaliatory threats, adding yet another option to counteract attacking forces. From a military point of view, it also makes a difference if the attacks are being directed against static facilities, such as air bases, as opposed to mobile units.

The type of weapon mounted on a ballistic missile also plays a role in determining the most appropriate countermeasure. A missile armed with high explosives is clearly different from one armed with an atomic device. Even conventional warheads can differ in character, however. A unitary warhead, which consists of one large explosive charge, differs significantly from a more sophisticated warhead armed with cluster munitions, minelets, brilliant munitions, or fuel air explosives. Similarly, missiles armed with chemical or biological weapons pose yet another type of problem.

It is the interplay of such factors that will determine the types of countermeasures likely to be adopted. It must be realized, however, that the search for response to the threat is a continuing process. Moreover, it is a process that requires innovation by Third World countries, because NATO and Warsaw Pact military powers have deliberately downplayed the problem.

Destruction of Missile Launchers

Tactical ballistic missiles can be destroyed on the ground before they are launched. This course might entail attacks on missile storage facilities or strikes against missiles mounted on launchers.[73] Under some circumstances, attacks on missile launchers may involve preemptive strikes designed to destroy missiles in the opening stages of a conflict. Preemptive destruction would be the conventional equivalent to the counterforce first strike discussed by nuclear strategists. It is an ideal way of protecting against ballistic missiles because it guarantees that the missiles cannot be used once hostilities get under way.

For a variety of reasons, however, it may not be possible to employ preemptive attacks. There may be insufficient warning of an impending attack, or political circumstances may make it impossible to adopt such a course of action. Moreover, during a protracted conflict, such as the Iran-Iraq War, the opposing sides will have sufficient time to replace any launchers lost during the opening stages of the fighting.

Destruction of missile launchers may not be easy to accomplish. The operational problems inherent in locating and attacking missile launchers are quite severe, and any defense based solely on destruction of launch vehicles must be considered suspect. Missiles of the type used in the Third World are transported and fired from highly mobile wheeled or tracked launcher vehicles (commonly known as TEL, for transporter-erector-launcher). The mobility of missile launchers makes it easy to move them from location to location.

Most countries give priority to the protection of their missile launchers. Syria, for example, reportedly keeps its TELs in specially constructed, fortified tunnels. The launchers leave the protected confines of these tunnels only when they are about to fire a missile.[74] Similarly, Saudi Arabia plans to store its DF-3 missiles in heavily fortified bunkers of Chinese design. These bunkers are based on the same designs used in China to protect the missiles from nuclear strikes, making them difficult to destroy with conventional ordnance. The Saudis may have more bunkers than they have launchers, so a potential adversary will never know the exact location of the missiles being stored.[75]

Missile launchers are easiest to find immediately after

firing because a missile can be detected in flight and its firing location determined. Standard military doctrine, however, requires that firing locations be surveyed well in advance, so that the launch vehicle can drive up to the spot and immediately initiate preparations for firing. TELs are intended to remain at a launch site only long enough to fire a single missile. As soon as the missile is fired, the launching vehicle is supposed to move to another location. Thus, to attack the TELs immediately after detection of a missile launch would require that a counterstrike be mounted within only a few minutes.

To attack launchers requires that TELs be distinguished from tens of thousands of other vehicles on the battlefield. Although it can be assumed that a high priority will be given to the detection of missile launchers, it will not be easy to find and destroy them in the short period of time available. Remotely piloted vehicles equipped with cameras can fly continuously above known missile storage bunkers to look for launching vehicles as they leave to fire their missiles, but even this technique may not be foolproof. Decoy trucks identical in appearance to real launch vehicles could be built, smoke and other screening systems could mask the storage facilities from external observation, and the missiles could be fired at night to limit the ease with which the movement of the launchers could be observed.

Nor would it be easy to locate the missile launchers by monitoring potential launch sites. A country planning to employ ballistic missiles is likely to survey a large number of potential launch sites, and it may not be possible to monitor all of them. This problem becomes especially acute with long-range missiles, which can be fired at less than their maximum range; the size of the area from which the missile can be fired is likely to be too large to keep under surveillance. Thus, even with modern intelligence collection methods and sophisticated munitions, it will probably not be possible to detect TELs reliably and attack them in transit.[76]

The number of Third World countries with the resources and the sophistication to create such an intelligence system is rather small. At present, the only country known to have such capabilities is Israel. Other countries are likely to find themselves in the situation faced by Israel in 1973: Israeli intelligence was unable to spot Syrian FROG-7 rocket launchers that were firing missiles from sites less than a mile from the front lines.[77]

Even if it is possible to locate the launchers, however, it will not be easy to destroy them. The air strike is the most likely method of attacking launchers because it is currently the only system with the accuracy and flexibility required to attack mobile targets of this type. Yet the amount of time required to organize and equip a force of attacking aircraft and the time needed to fly from an air base to the target area may be too long—especially when missiles of great range are involved. A missile fired from Iraq may take only seven or eight minutes to reach Israel, but an air strike from the opposite direction would take more than a hour. By that time, it is unlikely that the launcher is anywhere near the site from which the missile was fired. The problem is less acute for short-range missiles, but the inherent difficulty of hitting the launcher before it moves is not eliminated. Although it may take only five minutes for a high performance aircraft to fly only 100 kilometers, this interval should be sufficient to allow a well-trained crew of a TEL to be on the road away from the launch site.

The difficulties have been further increased by the proliferating number of missile launchers now being deployed. The Soviet Union supplies its clients with large numbers of launchers. The Syrians now have more than 50 surface-to-surface missile launchers (and an army of 9 divisions, or about 6 launchers a division) and may have more than 70 within a few years (or more than 8 launchers a division). Similarly, the Iraqis are believed to have more than 48 missile launchers.[78]

This proliferation of launchers makes the destruction of any one launcher relatively unimportant because the launchers can be used to fire more than one missile. Although destroying launchers would tend to limit the number of missiles that could be fired at any one time, so long as some launchers remain, it is possible to launch missiles until inventories of missiles are totally depleted. Destruction of launchers would not eliminate reserve missiles. Thus, to stop all missile attacks, it would be necessary to put every single launcher out of action and destroy all available missiles as well.

Retaliation

At least four countries in the Third World have explicitly adopted military doctrines that rely on the threat of retaliatory strikes as a means of deterring missile attacks. Among the countries that have enunciated such policies are Iran, Iraq, Israel, and Saudi Arabia. Both Iran and Saudi Arabia claim to have created their missile forces specifically for this role.

The Iranians appear to have built up their missile forces in part as a retaliatory response to Iraqi attacks on Iranian cities. Certainly, Iran's leaders appear to have no illusions that they can win the war by firing missiles at Iraqi cities. There has been no expectation on the part of Iranian leaders that Iran's ballistic missile forces alone would lead to an Iraqi defeat. The Iranians do believe, however, that a powerful missile force can act to deter Iraqi aircraft or missiles from striking their cities.[79]

Similarly, Israeli military officials have made it clear that attacks against populated areas will provoke immediate retaliatory strikes against economic and political targets. This policy was first developed during the 1973 Arab-Israeli War. During the first few days of the war, Syria fired FROG rockets at air bases in northern Israel, but some missed and hit agricultural settlements instead. In response, Israel mounted a strategic bombing campaign against Syria, including attacks on oil storage tanks, the oil refinery at Latakia, and power stations. Fewer than 100 combat sorties were needed to inflict heavy damage on the Syrians. The Israelis are likely to retaliate in a similar fashion in a future conflict, striking critical economic and political facilities.[80]

It will be more difficult for the Israelis to retaliate in response to missiles fired from Iraq or Saudi Arabia. Most strategic targets in those two countries are located a considerable distance from Israel, making it harder to mount effective retaliatory strikes. Nevertheless, both countries possess a large number of vulnerable economic and military installations, and neither has sufficient strength to defend all potential targets from attack. As the Israelis demonstrated in 1981 during the attack on the Osirak nuclear reactor in Iraq, the Israeli Air Force has the ability to mount highly destructive raids against targets at a considerable distance.

Saudi Arabia and Iraq also have enunciated retaliatory doctrines to protect against missile attacks. A major justification for the Saudi purchase of DF-3A missiles from China was a desire to deter possible Iranian attacks. The Saudis apparently believed that they required missiles capable of retaliating in kind to create a credible response to Iran's growing missile forces. Similarly, the government of Iraq indicated that its employment of missiles during the later stages was linked to Iranian attacks on Iraqi cities. Use of missiles was seen as the most effective means of compelling the Iranians to stop artillery, rocket, and missile strikes. Because many Iraqi cities were close to the front lines, Iraq was particularly vulnerable to city bombardment, whereas most major Iranian cities were far from the battle areas. Ballistic missile attacks were seen as a means of compensating for such geographic inequalities.

As the Iran-Iraq War demonstrates, retaliatory strikes may not prevent attacks on urban areas if the enemy is not willing to be deterred. Hence, there is a danger, as has happened during the Gulf War, that retaliatory strikes will degenerate into a vicious War of the Cities in which each side tries to inflict heavy damage on the opposition.

Hardening of Facilities

The effectiveness of conventional munitions attacks can be severely reduced by placing facilities likely to be attacked in fortified bunkers. Thus, the vulnerability of air bases can be minimized by putting aircraft, repair facilities, fuel and ammunition depots, and command posts into concrete shelters, preferably underground.[81] The same can be done with other types of facilities as well.

Not all military targets can be thus protected. Many military targets cannot be hardened and would continue to be vulnerable to missile strikes. Certain critical rear area facilities are particularly vulnerable. Equipment storage sites, support facilities, and defense factories cannot easily be protected behind concrete. Some military systems also are open to attack. Radar and surface-to-air missile sites, both likely targets of surface-to-surface missile attacks, cannot be fortified to any great extent.

Some countries have special vulnerabilities. Israel maintains large depots filled with the equipment used by reserve units. It would be impossibly expensive to replace these open air depots with underground storage sites or reinforced concrete buildings. For these reasons, passive defenses are only a partial solution to the threat of ballistic missiles.

Civil Defense

A number of countries have attempted to develop civil defense systems to protect civilians from missile attacks. Buildings can be fitted with bomb shelters, and the entire population can be provided with gas masks and other chemical defensive gear. Such measures can minimize casualties, but may not reduce them to acceptable levels. The speed with which missiles travel provides little warning time, and many people invariably will be caught unaware in the case of attack. In addition, missiles may penetrate conventional bomb shelters, which are not designed to stop massive objects traveling at supersonic speeds.

Although it may be possible to protect certain military facilities against missile attacks, it is not evident that shelters can protect civilians from ballistic missiles. The British discovered during World War II that bomb shelters built in building basements were useless in protecting civilians from V-2 missiles. Not only was there too little warning time to enable civilians to reach shelters, but even when they did, the impact of a supersonic missile with a 1-ton warhead was such that it penetrated several feet underground and created a crater 30 feet in diameter.[82] A missile such as the SS-21 takes only three to four minutes to reach its target, providing even less opportunity for civilians to reach bomb shelters before missiles strike.[83]

Iran attempted to construct shelters for the civilian population of major cities during the War of the Cities in March and April 1988.[84] The success of these efforts was limited, partially because of the difficulties inherent in construction of large numbers of shelters in a short period of time.

Electronic Countermeasures

Weapons that rely on electronic sensors and communications are generally vulnerable to electronic countermeasures. Such countermeasures can deceive or disrupt the electronic systems necessary for the operation of the weapon. To receive orders and obtain target information, missile launchers must be linked into a command and control system. In addition, some ballistic missiles depend on weather radar to provide adjustments in the trajectories to compensate for atmospheric conditions that might reduce the accuracy of the missiles. The Soviet Union typically provides meteorological radar to support missile launchers exported to the Third World. In addition, some missile guidance systems rely on midcourse correction from ground stations. Other missiles may employ terminal guidance techniques.

In general, however, ballistic missiles are relatively immune to electronic countermeasures. The missiles are generally self-contained after launch, relying on sensors that do not require external input. As a result, the opportunities for use of electronic countermeasures are fewer than with other types of weapons.

Nevertheless, there are some circumstances in which ballistic missile systems might be vulnerable to electronic countermeasures. Communications links needed for command and control of missiles are obvious targets for electronic disruption. Weather radar may be an attractive target for deceptive countermeasures armed at reducing the quality of the meteorological data available to missile units. Finally, missiles that rely on terminal guidance techniques may be vulnerable to a variety of electronic countermeasures.

Israel is the only country in the Third World known to have investigated potential electronic countermeasures against ballistic missiles.[85] In general, however, countries in the Third World lack the resources to devise defenses of this type. Moreover, given severe limits on the effectiveness of electronic countermeasures in this context, there is little reason to divert resources to this option.

Active Defenses

At present, there are no operational weapon systems available to Third World countries that are capable of shooting down ballistic missiles. The missiles travel at such high velocities that existing surface-to-air missile (SAM) systems, designed to destroy manned aircraft, are only marginally capable of intercepting them. High surface-performance SAMs can be upgraded to provide limited antitactical ballistic missile (ATBM) capabilities, but the operational differences between ballistic missiles and aircraft are so great that dedicated ATBM systems may be essential. Improvements in technology have recently made it practical to consider development of ATBM weapons to intercept and destroy tactical missiles.[86]

An effective ATBM requires a highly sophisticated sensor system, which can detect and precisely track large numbers of incoming missiles at long ranges, as well as a weapon able to destroy the incoming missile. Various types of equipment could be used to meet these requirements. Sophisticated phrased-array radar will be needed to track multiple targets at the same time, and infrared sensors, possibly based in space, could be used to detect missile launches. Potential weapons include hypersonic missiles capable of rapid acceleration, high energy lasers, charged particle beams, or hypervelocity guns. Many of these technologies have not yet matured, and it is unclear whether some of them will even be viable. Development of ATBM systems will be technically difficult, as well as expensive.

A number of countries are now developing ATBMs. The United States is exploring several such systems, including an upgraded version of the Patriot missile and two experimental ATBM weapons – the high endoatmospheric defense interceptor (HEDI) and the flexible lightweight agile guided experiment (FLAGE).[87] The Soviet Union is believed to have some systems with limited ATBM capabilities. A number of European countries, including West Germany and France, are known to be exploring ATBM-related technologies. Third World countries also are interested in acquiring ATBM systems. At least two Middle Eastern countries, Iraq and Israel, have active ATBM programs.

Reports from Baghdad indicate that Iraq is developing the Al-Faw 1 missile for the ATBM role. During the fall of 1988, this missile successfully intercepted short and medium-range ballistic missiles.[88] The capabilities of the Iraqi system are as yet unknown, and some analysts are inclined to dismiss the claims as propaganda.

According to Iraqi analyses, the requirement for the

Al-Faw 1 was a direct result of the "great strategic effects" of Iranian and Israeli ballistic missiles. "Iraqi antimissile missiles have now guaranteed the neutralization of [the] missile and [the] removal of their effect in any forthcoming confrontation between the Arabs and their enemies."[89] Iraqi military analysts argue that the Al-Faw 1 ATBM will play a critical role in future conflicts. It will neutralize Iranian and Israeli missiles, protecting both civilian and military targets from destruction. Iraq also views the Al-Faw 1 as a potential defense against Israeli Jericho missiles armed with nuclear weapons. As one analyst noted, an effective defense against ballistic missiles "will greatly contribute to undermining the credibility of deterrence by enemy surface-to-surface missiles and will also secure general freedom of action for Arab states and armies in general and for Iraq in particular." Iraq already possessed an effective air defense that "can curb the role of the enemy air force" with its surface-to-air missiles and interceptor aircraft. The Al-Faw 1 will extend the defenses to include ballistic missiles and thus "reduce to a minimum their effects on Iraqi or Arab cities."[90]

Israel has the most sophisticated ATBM program in the Third World. Israeli interest in active defenses against tactical ballistic missiles has reflected a growing awareness that alternative methods of defense may no longer be satisfactory. The program involves several elements. Central to the effort is the Arrow missile system being developed by Israel Aircraft Industries relying on funds provided by the United States. The Arrow is a Mach 9 area defense missile intended to intercept missiles with ranges up to 1,000 kilometers. In addition, the Israelis are known to have explored point defense ATBM systems, including the AB series of missiles and some rail gun systems.[91] Even if elements of the Israeli ATBM effort are deployed, the ATBM system is unlikely to be available until the mid-1990s. Hence, for at least the next five years, the Israelis will have to rely mainly on other methods to deter or minimize the danger of missile attacks.

Conclusion

Active defenses against ballistic missiles require the development of new technologies; they can be devised, but no existing options are totally adequate. The cost of these defenses is often high and the reliability of the existing methods often suspect. Such problems with defensive measures are likely to force countries to rely on retaliatory strategies. Thus, the absence of viable defenses may intensify the proliferation of ballistic missiles by increasing the attractiveness of ballistic missile retaliatory forces.

5

Solutions and Options

The proliferation of surface-to-surface missiles poses strategic problems for the United States and its allies. The missiles directly threaten U.S. military forces, as well as bases located in regions of tension. Countries allied to the United States are vulnerable to missile attacks and, in some cases, have already fallen victim to such strikes. Missile proliferation is causing a global arms race in missiles that has a destabilizing effect on whole regions of the world.

For the first time, countries in the Third World are acquiring the ability to strike at targets at long distances without worrying that defenses might intercept and destroy the attacking forces. The U.S. military has no weapons capable of intercepting ballistic missiles, and not until the early 1990s will even rudimentary defenses of this type come to be available. As Third World countries acquire accurate long-range surface-to-surface missiles, U.S. military installations around the globe will become increasingly vulnerable to attack.

The United States already has been the target of one missile attack. In 1986, Libya fired at least two Soviet-built Scud-B missiles at U.S. installations on the Italian island of Lampedusa. Fortunately, the missiles fell just short of the island, and no damage was done.[92] The missiles were launched in retaliation for the air raid on Libya.

This episode highlights an aspect of this problem all too often ignored in Washington. It is almost inevitable that in the future the U.S. military forces and installations will again be the target of long-range missiles fired by a Third World country. Some of the countries possessing ballistic missile forces are not only hostile to the United States but willing to employ force in pursuit of their policies. Such countries as Iran, Libya, North Korea, and Syria would hesitate little to use such missiles if it would serve their interests.

The missile threat to U.S. forces has emerged on a number of occasions during the past few years. In late 1984, U.S. military planners were concerned that Syrian SS-21 or Scud-B missiles might be used against U.S. forces operating in Lebanon. Similarly, U.S. forces in South Korea are now threatened by the Scud-B missiles being manufactured by North Korea.

Equally important, the missiles will pose a threat to countries that permit the basing of U.S. military forces. As more capable missile forces appear in the Third World, U.S. allies will have to take into account the danger of missile attacks. Does the United States know how its allies would have reacted to the 1986 Libyan raid if the Libyans had possessed long-range missiles? Almost certainly, the fear of Libyan attacks would cause many U.S. allies to distance themselves from the United States, especially if the missiles were to be armed with chemical warheads.

Libya will almost certainly try to acquire missiles with a range of 1,000 kilometers during the next decade and attempt to arm them with chemical agents. Accordingly, the United States must assume that Libya eventually will be able to fire missiles at targets throughout the Mediterranean region. A missile with a 1,000-kilometer range, if fired from Libya, can reach targets in Italy as far north as Rome. Israel's major cities will be just within reach. All of Greece and Egypt, as well as parts of Turkey, also will be threatened.

Countries friendly to the United States also are vulnerable to missile attacks, even in the absence of U.S. facilities. Afghanistan has fired Scud-B missiles at Pakistan and has threatened to escalate its strikes in retaliation for Pakistani support of Afghan guerrillas. Israel was attacked by missiles during the 1973 Arab-Israeli War. Other countries that might be targeted in the future include Saudi Arabia and South Korea.

Finally, the missiles destabilize the international environment. As additional countries acquire missiles and as the quality of the missiles improves, the international system becomes less stable. An arms race can emerge that has potentially dangerous consequences for all those affected. Countries that might be the targets of missile attacks have little time to develop responses to new developments.

It is ironic, therefore, that at the same time that Third World countries seek to acquire and make use of surface-to-surface missiles, the two superpowers have agreed to reduce their own inventories. The INF treaty, signed in 1987, obligates the Soviet Union and the United States to destroy their intermediate-range missiles. In many cases, Third World countries have sought to obtain missiles of the type that the Soviet Union and the United States are now eliminating.

U.S. Policy

Missile proliferation became an increasingly important issue during the last years of the Reagan administration. It continues to be a major concern for the Bush administration. During the 1988 presidential campaign, President George Bush stated, "The transfer of modern chemical and missile technology could give aggressive governments with terrorist records a new and terrifying potential: ballistic missiles armed with chemical warheads."[93] When Bush became president, efforts to stem the spread of surface-to-surface missiles were made a top priority, as reflected in the numerous statements made by his subordinates.[94]

The core of U.S. policy is the Missile Technology Control Regime (MTCR), adopted in April 1987 by the United States and six allied countries (Canada, France, Great Britain, Italy, Japan, and West Germany). The MTCR is not a treaty. Rather, it is a voluntary agreement between the signatories "to limit the risks of nuclear proliferation by controlling [technology] transfer that could make a contribution to nuclear weapons delivery other than manned aircraft."[95]

The MTCR attempts to control the development of rocket systems or unmanned air vehicles that have a range of 300 kilometers or more and can carry a payload of 500 kilograms or more. It prohibits the transfer of complete systems, components that could be used to produce a complete system, as well as the technology involved in the production of components and complete systems.

The road to the MTCR, however, appears to have begun in the waning days of the Carter administration, when certain U.S. officials became concerned that Third World countries were attempting to build surface-to-surface missiles. These concerns intensified under the Reagan administration. In 1981, it was discovered that "attempts were being made to purchase U.S.-origin missile components on a part-by-part basis."[96] As a result of interagency discussions, President Ronald Reagan signed National Security Decision Directive number 70 (NSDD 70) in November 1982.[97] There were two practical results of NSDD 70. First, the United States initiated negotiations that culminated in the MTCR in 1987, a process that took roughly four years. Second, in 1985, the U.S. government informally began to scan export licenses to prevent foreign sales of sensitive missile technology.[98]

Unfortunately, the policy options available to the United States are severely constrained. The proliferation of ballistic missiles is well advanced. A considerable number of countries already possess missiles, and their inventories often are quite substantial. Thus, there is no longer any question of keeping the missiles out of the hands of the Third World. Nor is it possible to prevent the indigenous production of missiles. A growing number of countries possess the technology to design and manufacture ballistic missiles. Even countries that lack the necessary technology can acquire it from foreign sources.

The demand for missiles is likely to remain intense because it is based on strategic and operational military requirements. In some instances, ballistic missiles are viewed as necessary elements of a strategic deterrence that includes chemical or nuclear weapons. In other cases, even conventionally armed missiles are thought to enhance deterrence against certain threats. Alternatively, missiles have operational military roles, substituting for small or ineffective air forces or acting as useful complements. Whatever the motivation, as long as ballistic missile forces are believed to enhance security, proliferation will continue.

An additional limitation on efforts to stem missile proliferation is the involvement of countries hostile to the United States. Some important suppliers are adversaries of the United States, as is the case with North Korea and the Soviet Union. Although the Soviet Union might be induced to cooperate in efforts to stem proliferation, the prospect of North Korea limiting missile exports is not favorable. Many of the more important recipients of missiles also are unfriendly toward the United States, including Iran, Libya, and Syria. It is unlikely that the United States will be able to influence the behavior of such countries.

Almost as problematic, however, are the allies of the United States, including South Korea, Saudi Arabia, and Israel. The United States has considerable interest in maintaining close relations with all of these countries, and all have legitimate security concerns that need to be taken into account. It may be difficult, even unwise, to persuade these countries to restrain their missile programs unless progress is made in restraining the activities of their adversaries.

Little would be gained by taking actions that might under-mine the security of friendly countries.

Criteria for Action

Existing realities constrain U.S. policy. At the same time, the dangers posed by the missiles are sufficiently acute to warrant an effort to constrain proliferation. To constrain proliferation, the United States needs to work closely with a wide variety of countries, many of whom have little interest in dealing with the problem.

The focus should be on slowing the pace of prolifera-tion. The United States should have no illusions that it can eliminate missile forces in the Third World, but it can make acquiring and building missiles more difficult. By increas-ing the amount of time required to deploy missile forces, some of the deleterious effects of the current missile race can be minimized.

It is likely that increasing diplomatic and economic costs will lead to the cancellation of some missile programs. If missile acquisition is made more expensive, other mili-tary requirements will compete for limited resources availa-ble for weapons procurement. Under such circumstances, missile programs are apt to be eliminated or given reduced priority. Higher costs also will affect the international trade in missiles by making purchases more expensive and less reliable.

Thus, the thrust of U.S. policy should be to increase the cost of missile proliferation, not to halt the proliferation of technology. There is no evidence that export controls can prevent technology transfer, even when rigorously enforced. Such controls can slow down the process and increase the costs, however.

Greater resources need to be devoted to monitoring and regulating missile proliferation. Although missile prolifera-tion has become a major concern, resources devoted to the problem are not commensurate with the extent of the problem.

Ultimately, the United States must accept that the world is becoming an increasingly dangerous place. It will be harder to protect allies from attack, and the risks entailed in military operations in the Third World are likely to grow.

Regional Approach

Certain U.S. officials have suggested that missile proliferation be handled on a regional basis. During the last months of the Reagan administration, the U.S. government appears to have initiated talks intended to deal with proliferation in the Middle East. This approach makes sense to the extent that proliferation is linked to regional developments.[99]

Bilateral Approach

The effort to stem missile proliferation has led to a large number of bilateral contacts with countries not members of the MTCR. Press accounts suggest that the United States has conducted such discussions with at least 10 countries. The most important of these contacts have been with the Soviet Union and China. The United States also has engaged in a variety of bilateral negotiations intended to address subjects of particular concern to the specific country involved.

The United States has conducted a series of high-level discussions with the Soviet Union. The exact nature of these talks remains unclear. Although the Soviet Union has indicated that it considers missile proliferation a serious problem, it has yet to accord it very high priority. It appears that the Soviets have agreed to abide by the provisions of the MTCR. In addition, there are indications that the Soviet Union may want to become a formal adherent to the regime.

There are some difficulties that will have to be overcome before the Soviets can be considered as fully participating in the MTCR process. The Soviet Union appears to believe that the Scud-B missile is not covered by the MTCR, because it has a range of just under 300 kilometers. In contrast, U.S. officials note that the Scud-B carries a large warhead and that a slight reduction in the payload would easily place the missile over the 300 kilometer threshold. Thus, the U.S. position is that the Scud-B should be included under the MTCR. The willingness of the Soviet Union to supply hundreds of missiles to Afghanistan suggests that it has an ambivalent attitude toward the problem. Nevertheless, the ongoing discussions have a potential significance that should not be ignored. Should the two superpowers reach agreement on a common, or at least coordinated, approach to missile proliferation, a considerable number of difficulties would be overcome.

China's supply of DF-3A missiles to Saudi Arabia led the United States to initiate talks with the Chinese on missile proliferation. During a 1988 visit to China, several senior U.S. officials indicated that the United States would like to see an end to Chinese ballistic missile exports. It was implied that continued exports of missiles might reduce U.S. willingness to transfer technology to China. In response, the Chinese apparently agreed to stop exports of missiles, although it is unclear whether these restraints applied to technology transfers as well.

Unfortunately, these efforts may be undermined by domestic events in China. The tension between the United States and China may reduce the willingness of China's leaders to pay attention to U.S. concerns. More concretely, the cancellation by the United States of trade agreements with China, including military technology transfers and contracts that would permit China to launch U.S.-built satellites, has eliminated incentives that provided the United States with critical leverage. Finally, China's financial distress, which will worsen as commercial links with the outside diminish, will increase incentives to sell weaponry to earn foreign exchange. Under such conditions, it should not be a surprise if China once again decided to export missiles.

Reducing Incentives to Proliferate

Countries in the Third World seek to acquire ballistic missiles to enhance security. Some analysts argue that unless these legitimate security concerns are taken into account, the MTCR will be a failure. From this perspective, the diplomacy required to implement the MTCR is likely to poison relations with friends, possibly damage their security, and yet not solve the overall problem of missile proliferation.[100]

Such a critique points out that the MTCR is discriminatory in its approach and has little legitimacy with countries in the Third World. It is a suppliers' agreement in which the members are free to transfer missiles and missile technology to each other, while attempting to prevent other countries from acquiring the same technology. Hence, it suggests that such countries as the United States, Britain, France, and West Germany have a legitimate use for missiles, but such Third World countries as Brazil, India, or Saudi Arabia do not. This view is unlikely to be acceptable to countries in the Third World. Hence, they are likely to evade the controls imposed by the MTCR.

It is possible to create nondiscriminatory agreements potentially acceptable to all countries. This approach was adopted by the proposed Chemical Weapons Convention (CWC) to prohibit all countries from producing or stocking chemical agents. Similarly, the provisions of the Non-Proliferation Treaty (NPT) apply equally to all its members (except the five major nuclear powers).

The MTCR also differs from other nonproliferation agreements by failing to offer incentives not to proliferate. A country that decides not to acquire missiles gains no advantage from its restraint. In contrast, the nuclear NPT offers access to nuclear technology if a country agrees to regulation of nuclear facilities.

These criticisms indicate the need for a policy that focuses primarily on solving the sources of tension that motivate countries to acquire ballistic missiles. In the case of the Arab-Israeli conflict, for example, the primary

objective should not be to force the participants to eliminate their missiles in the absence of alternative security
arrangements.

Many of these disputes are intractable, and many of
their origins date to the international order devised following World War II. A few are even older: Iran and Iraq have a
traditional antagonism that predates the national existence
of either country. It is unlikely that India and Pakistan will
come to terms with each other in the near future or that
North and South Korea will find a mutually acceptable res-
olution to their disagreements. Even under ideal circumstances, it might take decades before diplomatic solutions
resolve such interstate conflicts. During that interim period, proliferation is likely to continue unabated.

Moreover, even if diplomatic settlements are achieved,
it is unclear that the result would be a diminution in proliferation. Merely because two countries are at peace does not
prevent them from engaging in an arms race, as the United
States and the Soviet Union have clearly demonstrated during the past 40 years. Indeed, under some circumstances, it
is possible that countries may feel that missiles are needed
as a guarantee for peace, especially if a settlement might
require sacrifices that are believed to undermine security.

Strengthened Intelligence

The proliferation of missiles poses serious problems for U.S.
intelligence gathering. On a number of occasions, the United States has failed to detect significant developments. It
took U.S. intelligence at least two years to discover that the
Saudis had purchased the DF-3A from China, and the dis-
covery appears to have been largely accidental.[101] Similarly,
there is reason to believe that the United States was unaware of the magnitude of the Iraqi missile upgrade programs. As a result, it appears that U.S. policymakers were
surprised by the ability of Iraq to fire Al-Husayn missiles in
large quantities during the 1988 War of the Cities. Such

episodes question U.S. ability to monitor developments in missile proliferation.

Inhibiting Missile Proliferation

There is reason to believe that the Missile Technology Control Regime has worked. In several cases, the MTCR has derailed programs that otherwise might have been completed. It has also restrained some countries from exporting missiles.

The Condor missile program, long a source of concern in the United States and elsewhere, appears to be falling apart. Both Argentina and Egypt seem to be losing interest in the missile. The reasons are obvious: the financial burden of the Condor continues to escalate, severe technical difficulties remain unresolved, and the diplomatic costs are growing. The Condor depended heavily on the technical support provided by the West European companies, and that assistance has started to disappear.

These results would not have been possible without the framework provided by the MTCR. West European companies that once assisted such programs as the Condor now recognize that their activity has endangered far more lucrative U.S. defense contracts. Similarly, West European governments are starting to take seriously the need to regulate the activity of their nationals and to prevent them from exporting missile technology. Some countries with an interest in exporting missiles, such as Brazil and China, no longer appear to be actively marketing missiles. Their restraint is a direct result of U.S. initiatives.

The countries attempting to build ballistic missiles also have become acutely aware of U.S. efforts. Countries such as Argentina, Brazil, India, and Israel are aware that the United States seeks to limit the spread of ballistic missiles.

The success of these efforts can be attributed to the difficulties inherent in producing ballistic missiles, especially missiles with long ranges. There are a variety of reasons for such difficulties. Certain critical technologies appear especially difficult to master. Guidance systems are difficult to produce, and it seems doubtful that many countries will be able to develop their own guidance industries. Third World countries have had considerable difficulty producing the high-powered rocket motors for ballistic missiles. It also appears that they have had problems developing warheads and have required foreign assistance to make payloads of any sophistication.

Finally, it should be recognized that producing missiles is extremely expensive. It has been estimated that it will cost $3.2 billion to develop and produce 400 Condor missiles, or about $8 million per missile. Development costs alone may exceed $1 billion. Most Third World countries will have difficulty devoting such large amounts of money to projects of this sort.

For these reasons, many countries seeking to obtain ballistic missiles will have to be content to acquire complete systems from other Third World countries. Even countries that build their own missiles, however, almost certainly will use off-the-shelf components developed and built by other countries.

A comparison with fighter programs is probably appropriate. Only a few countries have attempted to develop their own high performance aircraft. It is generally recognized that buying aircraft from foreign sources makes more sense, even when the necessary technology is available. The cost of developing and producing an advanced fighter aircraft is high, the technological risks considerable, and the benefits relatively limited. When only a handful of companies in the entire world make high performance fighter engines, it is unlikely that a Third World country can easily do the same. As Third World countries better understand the difficulties of making ballistic missiles, they will likely regard ballistic missiles as they do fighter aircraft. At a certain point, many of these programs will be canceled, and countries will rely increasingly on shared missile technology.

There is a new aspect to the problem that is just beginning to emerge: the proliferation of cruise missiles. The technology to produce relatively inexpensive, accurate cruise missiles is becoming more widely available. In the 1990s, it is likely that a growing number of Third World countries will possess cruise missiles having long ranges and high accuracies.

Cruise missile guidance systems will be readily available, especially as commercial applications of the GPS become widespread. GPS systems make use of navigational signals transmitted by satellites. By using GPS receivers that cost only a few thousand dollars, it is possible for cruise missiles to achieve accuracies of less than 100 meters, even at long ranges. Moreover, taking advantage of the inexpensive technologies being developed for remotely piloted vehicles and drones should make it possible to build those missiles at relatively low cost. Tied together with cluster munitions, intelligent submunitions, and fuel air explosives, cruise missiles will have the accuracy and lethality to be extraordinarily effective.

It is the cruise missile that will pose the most serious challenge in the 1990s. The technology required to build conventionally armed cruise missiles will be within the reach of a considerable number of countries in the Third World.

Conclusion

By working with the other countries that have joined the MTCR and by conducting bilateral diplomacy with friendly countries in Third World, the United States should be able to slow the proliferation of ballistic missiles. The success of U.S. efforts will depend in part on the cooperation of the Soviet Union and China, but the United States should resist the temptation of trying to get these two countries to join the MTCR. For different reasons, both countries are likely to have problems with the regime, and, at this time,

U.S. diplomatic efforts could be better expended in bilateral discussions that are likely to lead to immediate results.

Thus, there is reason to be optimistic that the current proliferation of ballistic missiles can be brought under some kind of control. This optimism does not extend to cruise missiles, however. The technology required to make a cruise missile is easier to master and more readily available. The development and production costs are probably lower. Many of the technologies have legitimate civilian applications for small aircraft. As a result, it is likely that in the 1990s, a large number of countries in the Third World will begin to acquire relatively sophisticated cruise missiles.

Appendix

The terminology used to discuss surface-to-surface missiles is often confusing. Moreover, the standard definitions are often unhelpful in distinguishing between missiles with radically different characteristics. Ballistic missiles are powered by rockets while ascending, but are unpowered while descending. For purposes of this study, a ballistic missile is considered to be any ground-to-ground rocket or missile with a range of 40 kilometers or more.

Missiles require guidance systems, but some unguided surface-to-surface rockets are often considered to be ballistic missiles. Examples are the Soviet FROG-7, the U.S. Honest John, and the Iranian Oghab rockets – all of which are called missiles even though they have no guidance. Experience suggests that artillery rockets with long ranges can be used in much the same way as ballistic missiles. During the Iran-Iraq War, rockets such as the Soviet FROG-7 and the Iranian Oghab had sufficient range to strike cities located near battle areas. Both Iran and Iraq employed these rockets as strategic weapons. Because the long-range artillery rockets can be used in the same roles as ballistic missiles, they are treated together in this study.

Ballistic missiles are commonly classified according to range. The following distinctions are the ones adopted by the U.S. Department of Defense. A missile with a range of less than 600 nautical miles (1,100 kilometers) is a short-range ballistic missile (SRBM). A medium-range ballistic missile (MRBM) has a range of 600 to 1,500 nautical miles (1,100 to 2,750 kilometers). A missile with a range of 1,500 to 3,000 nautical miles (2,750 to 5,550 kilometers) is an intermediate-range ballistic missile (IRBM). An intercontinental ballistic missile (ICBM) has a range of 3,000 to 8,000 nautical miles (5,550 to 14,800 kilometers).[102]

Different distinctions were adopted during the negotiations between the United States and the Soviet Union on the Intermediate-Range Nuclear Forces (INF) Treaty. That agreement covers all surface-to-surface missiles with ranges of 500 to 5,000 kilometers. Thus, according to U.S. definitions, it includes short-range and medium-range missiles along with intermediate-range systems.

To complicate matters further, the Missile Technology Control Regime covers any missile with a range of at least 300 kilometers and a payload of 500 kilograms or more. This creates yet another categorization of missiles that fails to correspond to any of the existing classification systems.

Notes

1. For purposes of this study, surface-to-surface missiles are ballistic missiles and cruise missiles fired from the ground at targets on the ground. Included in this definition are artillery rockets with ranges of 40 kilometers or more. Excluded are anti-ship cruise missiles, such as the French Exocet or the Chinese Silkworm, and stand-off air-to-ground missiles. A more extended discussion of terminology appears in the Appendix.

When missiles are mentioned in the text without other qualifications, it should be assumed that surface-to-surface missiles are being discussed, not such other kinds as air-to-surface, surface-to-air, air-to-air, etc.

2. For purposes of this study, the Third World includes the economically developing countries of Asia, Africa, and South America. Excluded are developing countries in Europe, including Greece and Turkey. Twenty-two countries are the particular focus of this study: Afghanistan, Algeria, Argentina, Brazil, Cuba, Egypt, India, Indonesia, Iran, Iraq, Israel, Kuwait, Libya, North Korea, North Yemen, Pakistan, Saudi Arabia, South Africa, South Korea, South Yemen, Syria, and Taiwan.

3. For a discussion of the definition of a ballistic missile, see Aaron Karp, "Ballistic Missile Proliferation in the Third World," *World Armaments and Disarmament: SIPRI Yearbook 1989* (New York: Oxford University Press, 1989), 288.

4. Based on figures cited by Kenneth P. Werrell, *The Evolu-*

tion of the Cruise Missile (Washington, D.C.: Government Printing Office/Air University Press, September 1985), 60–61.

5. Among the best accounts of the Saudi missile sale was David Ottaway, "Saudis Hid Acquisition of Missiles," *Washington Post*, March 29, 1988, p. A13.

6. William H. Webster, director of the Central Intelligence Agency, in testimony on nuclear and missile proliferation before U.S. Senate, Committee on Governmental Affairs, May 18, 1989, p. 14.

7. See a map prepared by Leonard Spector, "Emerging Nuclear Weapons Nations 1989" (Carnegie Endowment for International Peace), which was shown at hearings held by U.S. Senate, Committee on Government Operations, May 18, 1989.

8. Ottaway, "Saudis Hid Acquisition of Missiles," A1; Jim Mann, "U.S. Caught Napping by Sino-Saudi Missile Deal," *Los Angeles Times*, May 4, 1988.

9. Remarks by William H. Webster, director of the Central Intelligence Agency, before the Town Hall of California, Los Angeles, California, March 30, 1989, p. 6.

10. Ibid.

11. William H. Webster, testimony on nuclear and missile proliferation before U.S. Senate, p. 7.

12. Interview on Tehran Television Service [in Farsi], March 28, 1988, as reported in Foreign Broadcast Information Service, *Daily Report: Near East and South Asia*, March 29, 1988, pp. 56–57.

13. Tehran IRNA [in English], March 29, 1988, as reported in Foreign Broadcast Information Service, *Daily Report: Near East and South Asia*, March 30, 1988, p. 48.

14. David Ottaway, "U.S. Increasing Arms Flow to Afghan Resistance," *Washington Post*, July 16, 1989, p. A24.

15. For a discussion of Syrian missiles, see Joseph S. Bermudez, Jr., "The Syrian Missile Threat," *Marine Corps Gazette*, January 1985, pp. 54–62.

16. Unless otherwise noted, all the material mentioned in this chapter was drawn from Aaron Karp (author of a number of published articles on missile proliferation), "Ballistic Missile Proliferation in the Third World," *World Armaments and Disarmament: SIPRI Yearbook 1989* (New York: Oxford University Press, 1989), and Congressional Research Service (CRS), Library of Congress, *Missile Proliferation: Survey of Emerging Missile Forces,*

CRS Report for Congress, October 3, 1988, as revised February 9, 1989.

17. Afghanistan, Algeria, Cuba, Egypt, Iraq, Kuwait, Libya, North Yemen, South Yemen, and Syria have received missiles directly from the Soviet Union. In addition, Iran and North Korea were provided Soviet-made missiles by third countries. Algeria may no longer have any missiles in inventory. This list is drawn from Karp, "Ballistic Missile Proliferation in the Third World," and CRS, *Missile Proliferation*.

18. Ottaway, "U.S. Increasing Arms Flow to Afghan Resistance," A24.

19. See the commentary by Reuven Pedatzur, "Military Involvement as a Political Tool," *Ha'aretz* [in Hebrew] as reported in Foreign Broadcast Information Service, *Daily Report: Near East*, July 29, 1987, p. L4.

20. Data from author interview with government official; not for attribution.

21. Vladimir Markov, "Establishing Control over the Exports of Missiles," *Novosti*, May 24, 1988.

22. Robert Pear, "U.S. Asserts Soviet Advisers Are Fighting in Afghanistan," *New York Times*, October 10, 1989, p. A17.

23. By the early 1970s, West Germany and Britain had obtained Sergeant missiles, and Honest John rockets were operated by Belgium, Britain, Denmark, Greece, Italy, and Turkey. Currently, West Germany operates Pershing 1A missiles, and Belgium, Britain, Italy, the Netherlands, and West Germany have Lance missiles. Only Greece and Turkey still retain the Honest John.

24. W. Seth Carus and Joseph S. Bermudez, Jr., "Iran's Growing Missile Forces," *Jane's Defence Weekly*, July 23, 1988, p. 130.

25. "China's M11 Is Revealed," *Jane's Defence Weekly*, April 9, 1988, p. 655; Edward Neilan, "Chinese Arms Trade Prompts Military to Seek Role in Politics," *Washington Times*, July 14, 1988, p. A7; Ihsan A. Hijazi, "Arab Lands Said to Be Turning to China for Arms," *New York Times*, June 24, 1988, p. A3.

26. By late 1988, the Chinese had stopped showing M-series missiles at arms shows. See the comments in Wen Po, "China's Missiles of a New Type on Display in Beijing," *Hsin Wan Pao* [in Chinese], as translated by Joint Publication Research Service, *Translations on Asia*, JPRD-TAC-88-043, November 29, 1988, p. 2.

27. William H. Webster, testimony on nuclear and missile proliferation before U.S. Senate, p. 9.

28. Bruce A. Smith, "Koreans Seek Military Air Challenges," *Aviation Week and Space Technology*, October 22, 1979, p. 63, reports that solid state electronics were fitted, along with "improved conventional warhead munitions." Normally, this phraseology is used to refer to a cluster munition warhead.

29. Robert Karniol, "Taiwan's Missile and Air Defence Developments," *Jane's Defence Weekly*, July 18, 1987, p. 84. It is suspected that the missile may be a copy of the Lance, which was built using pirated technology. Some of the technology may have been acquired by scientists and engineers working in the United States. In the mid-1970s, a large number of engineers from Taiwan were trained in the United States in missile technologies. See Edward Schumacher, "Taiwanese Program at MIT Ended," *Washington Post*, July 16, 1976, p. 5. In addition, there were allegations of Israeli assistance. See Melinda Liu, "Propping Up a Fading Friendship," *Far Eastern Economic Review*, October 27, 1978, p. 18. Israel had just received the Lance, so it had access to the technology.

30. David B. Ottaway, "Israel Reported to Test Controversial Missile," *Washington Post*, September 16, 1989, p. A17.

31. Carus and Bermudez, "Iran's Growing Missile Forces," 126–131, provides a comprehensive survey of the Iranian efforts to produce missiles.

32. According to William H. Webster, director of the Central Intelligence Agency, "In the mid-1960s, the U.S. accepted a young Indian scientist, Dr. Kalam, into a training program at the Wallops Island Rocketry Center. This scientist returned to India, and, with the knowledge gained from his work on the civilian space program, Dr. Kalam became the chief designer of India's Prithvi and Agni ballistic missiles." See testimony on nuclear and missile proliferation before U.S. Senate, Committee on Governmental Affairs, May 18, 1989, p. 12.

33. *O Glopo*, January 26, 1987, as translated by the British Broadcasting Corporation, *Summary of World Broadcasts, Part 4: The Middle East, Africa, and Latin America*, February 17, 1987, p. ME/W1428/A3/4.

34. "Iraq Seeking New SSMs," *Defense and Foreign Affairs Weekly*, May 25, 1987, p. 2. The reports that Iraq financed the SS-300 appear to have been incorrect.

35. Roberto Godoy, "Libyan Military Delegation's Visit to Brazil," *O Estado de Sao Paulo* [in Portuguese], January 22, 1988, p. 2, as translated by the British Broadcasting Corporation, *Summary of World Broadcasts, Part 4: The Middle East, Africa, and Latin America*, January 26, 1988, p. ME/0058/D/1; "Brazil Developing Ballistic Missiles," *Defense and Foreign Affairs Weekly*, January 19, 1987, p. 4.

36. Serge Schmemann, "West Germany Suspends Development of Missile," *New York Times*, February 9, 1989, p. A13.

37. Details can be gleaned from Karl Gunther Barth and Rudolf Lambrecht, "How German Scientists Developed a New Medium-Range Missile for Egypt and Argentina That Can Carry Nuclear Warheads," *Stern* [in German], August 25, 1988; "Several European Industries Involved in the International Web of the Condor Operation," *Corriere Della Sera* [in Italian], September 1, 1988; and BBC, "Panorama," April 10, 1989.

38. Barth and Lambrecht, "How German Scientists Developed a New Medium-Range Missile."

39. Steven M. Weisman, "Launching of a Satellite Rocket Fails in India," *New York Times*, July 14, 1988, p. A5.

40. Claudia Bensimon in *Jornal do Brasil* [in Portuguese], March 30, 1989, p. 20, reports that on March 27, 1989, a Brazilian company signed an agreement that provides it with access to Long March II rocket technology. The Long March II is China's main space launch vehicle.

41. Kyodo News Service [in English], March 9, 1989, as reported in Foreign Broadcast Information Service, *Daily Report: Near East and South Asia*, March 9, 1989, p. 48, states that China has agreed to help Iran build a factory capable of producing ballistic missiles with a range of 800 kilometers.

42. Joseph S. Bermudez, Jr. and W. Seth Carus, "The North Korean 'Scud B' Programme," *Jane's Soviet Intelligence Review*, April 1989, p. 178.

43. Bernard Trainor, "Pakistan Accused of Nuclear Move," *New York Times*, May 24, 1988, p. A1, reports that U.S. and Pakistani officials reported a Chinese connection with the Pakistani missile programs. Mushahid Hussain, "First Sight of Pakistan's 'Lance,'" *Jane's Defence Weekly*, March 11, 1989, p. 380, reports that the guidance package might have come from China.

44. Gerard Turbe, "Egyptian Rockets and the French Connection," *International Defense Review*, February 1988, p. 202.

45. "Several European Industries Involved in the International Web of the Condor Operation," *Corriere Della Sera* [in Italian], September 1, 1988.

46. Rome ANSA [in English], as reported in Foreign Broadcast Information Service, *Daily Report: Western Europe*, August 1, 1989, p. 10.

47. Bermudez and Carus, "The North Korean 'Scud B' Programme," 180.

48. Karp, "Ballistic Missile Proliferation in the Third World," 305–307, and Michael M. Gordon, "U.S. Says Data Suggests Israel Aids South Africa on Missile," *New York Times*, October 27, 1989, pp. A1, A7.

49. Seven countries have placed satellites into orbit: the Soviet Union (1957), the United States (1958), France (1965), China (1970), Japan (1970), India (1980), and Israel (1988). See Stuart Auerbach, "India Becomes Sixth Country to Put Satellite into Orbit," *Washington Post*, July 19, 1980. Only Japan does not make ballistic missiles for military purposes.

50. "South African Missile Test," *Jane's Defence Weekly*, July 15, 1989, p. 59.

51. Johannesburg *SAPA* [in English], May 30, 1989, as reported in Foreign Broadcast Information Service, *Daily Report: Africa*, June 8, 1989, p. 13.

52. John J. Fialka, "Space Research Fuels Arms Proliferation," *Wall Street Journal*, July 6, 1989, p. A8.

53. "Space, Upper Atmosphere Research Committee Upgraded," *Morning News* (Karachi), June 4, 1981, p. 3; B. Radhajrishna Rao, "A Military Option," *Nature*, December 10, 1981, p. 907.

54. Salim Mehmud, "Progress on Space Research in Pakistan," *Pakistan and Gulf Economist*, October 13–19, 1984, pp. 38–40; S. M. Fazal, "Future of Space Technology in Pakistan," *Pakistan and Gulf Economist*, May 15–21, 1982, pp. 11–13 (interview with Dr. Salim Mehmud, chairman of SUPARCO).

55. Islamabad Domestic Service [in Urdu], January 12, 1988, as reported in Foreign Broadcast Information Service, *Daily Report: Near East and South Asia*, January 13, 1988, p. 70.

56. Wolfgang Flume, "Air Defence in Central Europe," *Military Technology*, June 1986, p. 116.

57. Anthony Cordesman, *The Iran-Iraq War and Western Security 1984-1987* (New York: Jane's Publishing, 1987), 135.

58. Aharon Levran and Zeev Eytan, *The Middle East Mili-*

tary Balance 1987-1988 (Boulder, Colo.: Westview Press for the Jaffee Center for Strategic Studies, 1988), 165–167, 401–403.

59. Karl Schnell, "Experiences of the Lebanon War," *Military Technology*, July 1984, p. 32.

60. International Institute for Strategic Studies (IISS), *Military Balance 1988-1989* (London: Brassey's/IISS, 1988), 213.

61. Ibid., 215; Steven J. Zaloga and James W. Loop, *Soviet Tanks and Combat Vehicles 1946 to the Present* (London: Arms and Armour Press, 1987), 153.

62. Dan McKinnon, *Bullseye One Reactor* (San Diego, Calif.: House of Hits, 1987), 110–117.

63. These issues are discussed in W. Seth Carus, "Missiles in the Middle East: A New Threat to Stability," *Policy Focus*, Washington Institute for Near East Policy, Research Memorandum No. 6, June 1988.

64. "More Details of the Egyptian Sakr 80 Rocket System," *Jane's Defence Weekly*, March 12, 1988, pp. 462–463.

65. "Special Report: Iraqi Arms Production," *MEDNEWS: Middle East Defense News*, May 8, 1989, p. 8.

66. "India Enters the Missile Age," *Sunday*, March 13–19, 1988, p. 37.

67. Baghdad INA [in English], March 12, 1988, as reported in Foreign Broadcast Information Service, *Daily Report: Near East and South Asia*, March 14, 1988, p. 26.

68. These figure were compiled by the author in an unpublished study of the War of the Cities. Some of the data appears in Carus and Bermudez, "Iran's Growing Missile Forces," 126–130, and in an unpublished article, W. Seth Carus and Joseph S. Bermudez, Jr., "Iraq's Al-Husayn Missile Program."

69. Ottaway, "U.S. Increasing Arms Flow to Afghan Resistance," A24.

70. John D. Morocco, "LTV to Receive Army Contract for Initial ATACMS Production," *Aviation Week and Space Technology*, October 24, 1988, pp. 20–21; Charles Rabb, "ATACMS Adds Long-Range Punch," *Defense Electronics*, August 1986, pp. 69–75; Tom Donnelly, "LTV Ousts Boeing in Bid War for Army Tactical Missile," *Defense News*, March 31, 1986, p. 22; Tom Donnelly, "Army Allots $1 Billion for Deep Strike Missile," *Defense News*, March 10, 1986, pp. 1, 14.

71. "Agni Readying for Launch," *The Hindu* (New Delhi), July 14, 1988, p. 7, as reported in Foreign Broadcast Information Ser-

vice, *Daily Report: Near East and South Asia*, September 6, 1988, p. 39. This article suggests that when using new guidance technologies, an intermediate-range ballistic missile can be designed with a CEP of only 50 meters and that by using terminal guidance, it will be possible to reduce that to 1 to 3 meters.

72. IISS, *Military Balance 1988–1989*, p. 210.

73. This is the favored option of at least some U.S. defense experts. See Melissa Healy, "Army Must Take New Shot at an Anti-Tactical Missile," *Defense Week*, December 10, 1984, p. 3.

74. Bermudez, "The Syrian Missile Threat," 55, 60.

75. A description of the missile base at As-Sulayyil appears in "Satellite Captures First Views of Saudi CSS-2 Missile Sites," *Jane's Defence Weekly*, October 1, 1988, pp. 744–745.

76. Note the comments of U.S. defense officials on this very subject, but in a European context, as reported in Jack Cushman, "New Missiles: Grave Danger to NATO Bases," *Defense Week*, October 31, 1983, p. 13.

77. Bermudez, "The Syrian Missile Threat," 55.

78. Levran and Eytan, *The Middle East Military Balance 1987–1988*, pp. 213–217, 222–225, 301, 401.

79. Quoted in Carus and Bermudez, Jr., "Iran's Growing Missile Forces," 131.

80. *IDF Radio*, December 26, 1985, as quoted in State of Israel, Government Press Office (press release), December 26, 1985, quoted Yitzhak Rabin as follows: "The Arab states have in their possession missiles capable of achieving — without a capability of intercepting them — a strike at the large [Israeli] population centers. The other side must know, that for each attempted strike during a war indiscriminately against the civilian population, against civilian population centers, there will be a massive Israeli response, using the same various means against the other side's population centers."

81. The protection of Israeli air bases is discussed in W. Seth Carus, *The Threat to Israel's Air Bases*, AIPAC Papers on U.S.-Israeli Relations, No. 12 (Washington, D.C.: American Israel Public Affairs Committee, 1985), 43–47.

82. David Johnson, *V-1, V-2: Hitler's Vengeance on London* (New York: Stein and Day, 1981), 157–158.

83. Flume, "Air Defence in Central Europe," 116, gives the flight time of the SS-21.

84. Tehran Domestic Service [in Farsi], March 6, 1988, as

reported in Foreign Broadcast Information Service, *Daily Report: Near East and South Asia*, March 9, 1988, pp. 62–63.

85. Joshua Brilliant, "U.S. Star Wars Official Urges Israel to Join," *Jerusalem Post International Edition*, March 1, 1986, reports that Israel proposed U.S. funding for electronic countermeasures for use against ballistic missiles.

86. Manfred R. Hamm and Kim R. Holmes, "A European Antitactical Ballistic Missile System, Deterrence, and the Conventional Defense of NATO," *Washington Quarterly* 10, No. 2 (Spring 1987):67.

87. "Army/LTV Missile Intercepts Reentry Vehicle," *Aviation Week and Space Technology*, July 14, 1986, p. 119; Trish Gilmartin, "U.S. Army to Examine Existing Systems for Use against Tactical Ballistic Missiles," *Defense News*, April 20, 1987, pp. 3, 7.

88. Baghdad Domestic Service [in Arabic], November 30, 1988, as reported in Foreign Broadcast Information Service, *Daily Report: Near East and South Asia*, December 1, 1988, p. 29.

89. Staff Brigadier General Amjad Hasan al-Zuhayri (ret.), "The Al-Faw-1 Antimissile Missile and Its Strategic Value," *Al-Jumhuriyah* [in Arabic], December 19, 1988, p. 3, as reported in Foreign Broadcast Information Service, *Daily Report: Near East and South Asia*, December 27, 1988, pp. 21–22.

90. Ibid.

91. See W. Seth Carus, "NATO, Israel and the Tactical Missile Challenge," *Policy Focus*, Washington Institute for Near East Policy, Research Memorandum, No. 4, May 1987.

92. "Libyan Scud B Attack on Lampedusa Island," *Jane's Defence Weekly*, April 26, 1987, p. 739.

93. Speech at University of Toledo, Toledo, Ohio, October 21, 1988.

94. The subject has been discussed by Secretary of State James Baker, as well as lower ranking officials from the departments of State and Defense and the Arms Control and Disarmament Agency. One of the most articulate spokesmen, however, has been William H. Webster, director of the Central Intelligence Agency, who has repeatedly mentioned his concern about the proliferation of ballistic missiles. Note his testimony on nuclear and missile proliferation before the U.S. Senate, Committee on Governmental Affairs, May 18, 1989.

95. CRS, "Missile Proliferation," CRS-104.

96. Statement by Ambassador Ronald F. Lehman II, director, Arms Control and Disarmament Agency, on nuclear and missile proliferation before the U.S. Senate, Committee on Governmental Affairs, May 18, 1989.

97. The best single discussion of the MTCR is provided by Manoj Joshi (Madras), *The Hindu* [in English], November 3, 1988, p. 8.

98. Data from author's interview with government official (not for attribution). It appears that only the departments of Defense and State tried to prevent exports of missile technology before 1987. The Department of Commerce has indicated that it only initiated export controls after the MTCR went into effect on August 1, 1987.

99. Michael R. Gordon, "U.S. Urges Talks on Missiles in Mideast," *New York Times*, December 27, 1988, p. A3.

100. The following discussion is based on the testimony of Geoffrey Kemp before the U.S. Senate, Armed Services Committee, Subcommittee on Defense Industry and Technology, May 2, 1989.

101. Mann, "U.S. Caught Napping by Sino-Saudi Missile Deal," 1.

102. U.S. Department of Defense, Joint Chiefs of Staff, *Dictionary of Military and Associated Terms*, JCS Pub. 1, January 1, 1986. There are confusing variations on this scheme. The International Institute for Strategic Studies gives the following ranges: SRBM – under 800 kilometers; MRBM – 800 to 2,400 kilometers; IRBM – 2,400 to 5,500 kilometers; ICBM – more than 5,500 kilometers. See *Military Balance 1986-1987* (London: International Institute for Strategic Studies, 1986), 207.

Postscript

Recent events in the Middle East confirm the extent to which ballistic missile proliferation has become a national security problem for the United States. Until recently, the only ballistic missiles of concern to the United States were the ones in the inventories of the Soviet Union. Now, however, it is evident that other countries possess the means and the will to employ ballistic missiles against the United States and its close allies (see Tables 1–3 at the end of this chapter).

The War with Iraq

Iraq developed an extensive ballistic missile force during the last years of the 1980–1988 war with Iran. Initially, Iraq possessed only Soviet-supplied Scud-B missiles. By the end of the war, however, Iraq was firing Al-Husayn missiles, which were modified versions of the Scud with double the range. Baghdad continued to expand its missile force even after the end of the war with Iran in August 1988. As a result, by late 1990 Iraq was estimated to have more than 60 launchers, half static and the others mobile.

Its inventory of missiles was placed at between 300 and 1,000.

When the United States opened hostilities with Iraq in January 1991, Iraq's missile force almost immediately became an important factor. Iraq found that its expensively acquired air force was largely useless. Attacks on air bases and the continuous presence of hostile fighters made it virtually impossible for its aircraft to mount offensive strikes. As a result, Iraq's sole useful offensive instrument became its missile forces.

The importance of the missile forces resulted in large measure from the difficulties of locating and destroying launchers. In contrast to air bases, which are large, easy to locate, and vulnerable to attack, missile launchers are small, hard to find, and easy to disperse targets. As a result, it was possible for Iraq to launch scores of missiles but only a handful of aircraft sorties.

The attacks also demonstrated the key difference between military and strategic utility. Clearly, the inaccuracy and small warheads of the Iraqi missiles give them limited military value. Although many people were wounded, and many buildings made uninhabitable, the resulting deaths were few. Nevertheless, the strategic implications of the attacks were enormous. Iraqi efforts to involve Israel in the conflict, a strategy intended to disrupt the anti-Iraq alliance, depended mainly on the missile strikes. Iraq clearly hoped that Israel would retaliate, transforming the war into yet another Arab-Israeli conflict.

To stop attacks, the United States and its allies were forced to devote an unexpectedly large effort to locating and destroying Iraq's missile launchers. At the same time, the United States rushed U.S. Army Patriot surface-to-air missile batteries to protect Israel, primarily to avert Israeli retaliatory strikes.

In this fashion, the ability of the Patriots to intercept ballistic missiles assumed an unexpected strategic importance. Relatively simple upgrades to this surface-to-air missile made it capable of intercepting short-range ballistic missiles. This minimized the damage inflicted by the Iraqi ballistic missiles, thus substantially reducing the political impact of the attacks. Nevertheless, the Iraqi missiles caused damage because the Patriot missiles cannot easily destroy incoming missiles at a distance from the target area. As a result, debris and undamaged warheads remained a problem.

The relative successes of the U.S. Patriot has emphasized the importance of antitactical ballistic missile systems. It is likely that countries in the Third World will look to the Patriot, or to similar systems, to provide defenses against ballistic missiles. Some of these systems may originate in the Third World. Israel is developing the Arrow missile, Iraq claimed to be working on the Fao, and Taiwan claims to be working on a system as well.

Other developments are also of some interest. The U.S. Army has ATACMS surface-to-surface missiles in Saudi Arabia. This is the first combat deployment of this new generation missile and almost certainly will become its first test in battle. Unlike the Iraqi derivatives of the Soviet Scud, the ATACMS is a semi-ballistic missile. It can change its trajectory and velocity to meet tactical objectives, making it harder to intercept and potentially more dangerous to the target.

The Persian Gulf War also has seen the first employment of land attack cruise missiles since the German attacks on London in 1944. Initial reports indicate that U.S. Navy Tomahawk missiles launched from ships and submarines in the Persian Gulf and Indian Ocean hit strategically important targets with considerable accuracy. A number of countries in the Third World are known to be exploring cruise missile technology, and the performance of the Tomahawks is certain to further increase interest in such weapons.

In the end, it is likely that the events of early 1991 will increase interest in both ballistic and cruise missiles, as well as in defenses against those missiles.

Regional Developments

The dramatic events in the Persian Gulf should not lead us to forget that efforts to develop ballistic missiles continue in other parts of the world. Our information on missile development programs is often scanty, so that it is not possible to highlight recent trends for many countries. Nevertheless, certain general trends are evident.

The missile programs in Argentina and Brazil appear to have slowed for a combination of political and economic reasons. South Africa has now conducted at least two tests of rocket boosters that appear to have been based on the Israeli Jericho ballistic missile. The Israelis have continued to launch Jericho missiles into the eastern Mediterranean, suggesting that further enhancements to the missile are being made.

East Asia continues to be a center of missile development. North Korea has continued work on an extended-range version of the Scud and is believed to have discussed sales of the new missile to Syria. Taiwan has hesitated to initiate development of a space launch vehicle, which would have potential military applications. On the other hand, defense officials in Taiwan have admitted that its new generation of surface-to-air missiles were designed with surface-to-surface capabilities. Indonesia seems to be following the Brazilian model in its efforts to develop ballistic missiles, starting with long range artillery rockets and then moving on to larger missiles. In 1990, the Indonesian military adopted a locally designed artillery rocket with a range of 60 kilometers.

Technological Trends

The sophistication of missiles now under development is increasing, resulting in missiles with greater range, accuracy, and lethality. From this perspective, the Iraqi missiles are less dangerous than many of the Third World systems now under development or in service.

Of particular concern is the possibility that Third World countries might make use of satellite navigation systems to enhance the accuracy of missiles. The United States and the Soviet Union are now placing constellations of satellites in orbit to create a global navigation network. The Global Positioning System (GPS), created by the United States, can provide positional information within 15 meters of the actual location. These signals are available to commercial users, but only in a degraded form that ensures an accuracy of only 100 meters. The equipment is small and relatively inexpensive, costing only a few thousand dollars.

It is known that several Third World countries are investigating use of such systems. India has suggested that it intends to employ such receivers on future reentry vehicles. Israel and South Africa are known to produce small receivers for military use, and other Third World countries are certainly capable of doing so.

GPS is an example of a technology that Third World countries could develop to ease efforts to develop accurate, militarily useful missiles.

Stopping Missile Proliferation

Efforts to constrain ballistic missile proliferation continue to receive a high priority. Twelve countries are now full partners in the Missile Technology Control Regime. Besides the original seven countries, Spain, the three Benelux countries, and Australia are believed to be members. In addition, other countries have suggested that they intend to abide by provisions of the regime.

Even advocates of the regime, however, admit that it has important inadequacies. Not all countries capable of supplying missiles and missile technology are members.

China refuses to accept the regime, and no Third World country has joined.

Attempts have been made to define alternative approaches to the regime. There appears to be little interest in proposals to ban all ballistic missiles. Similarly, there appears to be little interest in a global extension of the U.S.-Soviet INF treaty, which banned missiles with ranges of 500 to 5,500 kilometers from the inventories of the two superpowers. It is possible that some new formulation might attract greater interest, but for now the prospects appear poor.

Efforts to constrain ballistic missile proliferation will meet with some successes, but will only slow the inexorable spread of these systems. As a result, it appears inevitable that the Third World countries gradually will acquire missiles of increasing range, improved accuracy, and enhanced lethality.

February 1991

TABLE 1
Third World Ballistic Missiles, Space Launch Vehicles, and Artillery Rockets (in service and under development)

Country	Foreign Missiles/Rockets	Indigenous Missiles/Rockets	Space Launchers
Afghanistan	Scud B		
Algeria	FROG-7 ?		
Argentina		Alacran ?; Condor IA; Condor 2	
Brazil		ASTROS II; SS-300/1000; MB/EE-150/350/600/1000	SLV
Cuba	FROG-7		
Egypt	FROG-7; Scud B	Sakr-80; Scud B ?	
India		Prithvi; Agni; Proposed ICBM; MBRS	SLV-3; ASLV; PSLV; GSLV
Indonesia		LAR/MAR; RX-250	Name not known
Iran	Scud B	Scud B ?; Tondar 68; Nazeat; Oghab	
Iraq	FROG-7; Scud B; ASTROS II/SS-60	Tammus 1; Al-Albbas; Al-Husayn; Fahd 600; Fahd 300; Ababil 100; Laith 90; Sajil 60; Ababil 50	Al Abid

(continued)

TABLE 1
Continued

Country	Foreign Missiles/Rockets	Indigenous Missiles/Rockets	Space Launchers
Israel	Lance	Jericho; MAR-290; MAR-350	Shavit
North Korea	FROG-7	Scud B; extended range Scud	
South Korea	Honest John	Honest John; NHK-1; South Korea SSM	Name not known
Kuwait	FROG-7		
Libya	FROG-7; Scud B; SS-21 ?	Fateh ?	
Pakistan	DF-3A	Hatf I; Hatf II; Hatf III ?	Name not known
Saudi Arabia			
South Africa		"Arniston"	Name not known
Syria	SS-21; Scud B; FROG-7		
Taiwan		Ching Feng ?; Tien Ma ?	Name not known
Yemen	FROG-7; Scud B; SS-21		

TABLE 2
Third World Short Range Ballistic Missiles
(in service or under development)

Producing Country	Designation	Status	Range (km)	Accuracy CEP (m)	Warhead Types	Third World Users
Argentina	Alacran	D	200	?		
Brazil	SS-300	D	300	?	high explosive; cluster ?	
	MB/EE	D	150	?	high explosive; cluster ?	
China	M-11	D	290	290 ?	high explosive; cluster ?	
	8610 ?	S	150	?	?	
Egypt	Scud B	D ?	300	1000		
India	Prithvi	D	250	250	high explosive; cluster; minelet; fuel air explosive	
Indonesia	RX-250 ?	D	?	?	?	
Iran	"IRAN-130"	S	120	?	high explosive	Iran
	"IRAN-160"	S	160	?	high explosive	Iran
	"IRAN-200"	S	200	?	high explosive	Iran
	Scud B	S ?	300–320	900		
Iraq	Fahd	D	250–300	?		Iraq

(continued)

TABLE 2
Continued

Producing Country	Designation	Status	Range (km)	Accuracy CEP (m)	Warhead Types	Third World Users
North Korea	Scud B	S	300–320	1000	high explosive; chemical	North Korea; Iran
South Korea	NHK-1	?	180	?	high explosive	South Korea
	Korean SSM	67	260	?	?	South Korea
Pakistan	Hatf II	D	300	?	?	Pakistan
Soviet Union	SS-21	S	100	100 ?	high explosive; cluster	Libya ?; Syria; North Yemen; South Yemen ?;
	Scud B	S	300	900	high explosive	Afghanistan; Egypt; Iraq; Libya; Syria; South Yemen
Taiwan	Ching Feng	S	100	?	?	Taiwan
United States	Lance	S	133	375	cluster	Israel

TABLE 3
Third World Short Range Ballistic Missiles
(in service or under development)

Producing Country	Designation	Status	Range (km)	Accuracy CEP (m)	Warhead Types	Third World Users
Argentina	Condor II	D	900	900	high explosive; fuel air explosive	
Brazil	SS-1000	D	1200	?	?	
	MB/EE-350	D	350	?	?	
	MB/EE-600	D	600	?	?	
	MB/EE-1000	D	1000	?	?	
	Proposed IRBM	D	3000	?	nuclear	
China	M-9	D	600	600	?	
	DF-3A	S	3000	2500	high explosive	Saudi Arabia
Egypt	"Vector"	D ?	1000	750 ?	high explosive; fuel air explosive	
India	Agni	D	2500	2500 ?		
	"ICBM"	D	5000	50 ?		
Iran	M-9 ?	D ?	600	600		

(continued)

TABLE 3
Continued

Producing Country	Designation	Status	Range (km)	Accuracy CEP (m)	Warhead Types	Third World Users
Iraq	Al-Husayn	S	600	500	high explosive; chemical; biological	Iraq
	Al-Abbas	S	800	300	high explosive; chemical; biological?	Iraq
	Tammus 1	D	2000	?	?	Iraq
	Fahd	D	500–600	?	?	
Israel	Jericho I	S ?	480–560	?	nuclear; high explosive; chemical	Israel
	Jericho II	S	1500 ?	?	nuclear; high explosive; chemical	Israel
	Jericho IIB (III?)	D	2500	?	nuclear; high explosive; chemical	Israel
Libya	Fateh	D	500	?	?	
North Korea	Scud B PIP	D ?	600 ?	?	high explosive; chemical	
Pakistan	Hatf III (?)	D	600	?	nuclear ?	
South Africa	"Arniston"	D	1500	?	nuclear ?	
Taiwan	Tien Ma	D ?	960	?	?	

Index